THE LIFE AND LETTERS OF CAPTAIN JOHN O'BRIEN

Second in the Series:

"Early Lane County, Oregon Families with Lorane Connections"

By Pat Edwards

Sawdust and Cider; A History of Lorane, Oregon and the Siuslaw Valley (1987)
From Sawdust and Cider to Wine (2006)
OREGON'S MAIN STREET: U.S. Highway 99 "The Folk History" (2014)
The Baileys of Bailey Hill (2017)

Copyright © 2018
by Pat Edwards

All rights reserved. No part of the material protected
by this copyright notice may be reproduced or
utilized in any form or by any means, electronic or
mechanical, including photocopying,
recording or by any informational
storage and retrieval system
without written permission from the copyright owner.

1st Edition, 2018

Published by

Groundwaters Publishing, LLC
P.O. Box 50, Lorane, Oregon 97451
http://www.groundwaterspublishing.com

ISBN-13: 978-1720900078
ISBN-10: 1720900078

Acknowledgments

My sincere thanks go to John F.M. Dwyer who has so generously shared his many hours of family research and resources with me. John is the great-great grandson of Mary Walker, Capt. John O'Brien's favorite cousin who thoughtfully saved his letters from the Civil War.

The complete text of all of Captain John'O'Brien's letters in his family's possession will be included in a separate book assembled and presented under John Dwyer's name. It will include more of the O'Brien family history than I was able to use for this book.

Thank you, John! Your help has been invaluable.

PREFACE

In 1873 and 1874, after serving four years as a Union soldier in the Civil War, Captain John O'Brien homesteaded 160 acres of land south of Lorane, Oregon in what is now the Letz Creek Road area. The Homestead Act of 1862 provided free land to veterans who had served in the Civil War as well as others who qualified. Capt. O'Brien, however, didn't live there full time until 1907, when he retired as the President of the Multnomah Typographical Union #58 and stepped down from the International Federated Trades Assembly of Portland in which he took an active role for many years.

It was obvious that Capt. O'Brien loved his farm. He spent as much time there as possible, using it as a retreat from the rigors of running a trade union and a daily newspaper in the big city.

His story is rich in texture. A printer by trade, he was a man who lived his life as a leader, but proved also to be a gracious and gentle man. Much of the time he spent as a Union soldier during the Civil War, first as a private and eventually being promoted through the ranks to captain by brevet, is recorded in his own hand from the almost 50 letters he wrote to a favorite cousin throughout his four years of service.

After leaving the military at the end of the Civil War, he took up the cause of the men who worked in the trades—especially the printing trade—and he became deeply involved in setting up trade unions to make sure that the workers who mainly used their hands and training in helping to build America were treated fairly and provided a living wage for their families.

That vocation took him far from his Connecticut upbringing, first to Helena, Montana, then to Sacramento, California and soon, San Francisco, where he married his wife, Julia. He then settled in Portland, Oregon where he continued to champion the cause of the working man.

He was a man of substance and from the stories told about him in the Lorane area, especially, he was loved and respected by his neighbors, as well.

This book is the second in a series that showcases the lives of some of the very interesting early settlers in Lane County who had direct connections to the Siuslaw Valley and Lorane, specifically.

In 2017, I wrote the first book called *The Baileys of Bailey Hill* about a large family who first came to Lane County in the 1840s and 1850s. The Bailey Hill portion of Eugene, Oregon is named after them. One of the brothers, Thomas Bailey, took out a donation land claim near Lorane in what is now the area of Jackson-Marlow Road, a few miles north of Lorane, and several of his siblings and their families lived there at different times.

Some members of the family were volunteers in the Rogue River Indian Wars of 1855 and 1856 and two of the brothers lost their lives as a result.

The Printer and His Types
The Montana Post, Thursday, February 16, 1867

The following beautiful extract is from the pen of Benjamin F. Taylor, the printer poet. It contains a fund of information, and a wealth of pathos, clothed in language which cannot fail to excite both interest and admiration:

> Perhaps there is no department or enterprise whose details are less understood by intelligent people than the "art preservative"—the achievement of types.
>
> Every day their life long, they are accustomed to read the paper, and find fault with its statements, its arguments, its looks; to plume themselves upon the discovery of some roughish and acrobatic type that gets into a frolic and stands upon its head; or of some waste letter or two in it—but, of the process by which the newspaper is made, of the myriads of motion and of the thousands of pieces necessary to its composition, they know little and think less.
>
> They imagine they discourse of a wonder, indeed, when they speak of the fair white carpet, woven for thought to walk on, of the rags that fluttered on the back of the beggar, yesterday.
>
> But, there is something more wonderful still. When we look at the one hundred and fifty-two little boxes, somewhat shaded by the touch of inky fingers, that compose the printer's "case," noiseless except the clicking of the type, as one by one they take their places in the growing line—we think we have found the marvel of the art.
>
> We think how many fancies in fragments there are in the boxes; how many atoms of poetry and eloquence the printer can make here and there, if he

had only a little chart to work by, how many facts in a small "handful," how much truth in chaos.

Now, he picks up the scattered elements until he holds in his hands a stanza of "Gray's Elegy," or a monody upon Grimes' "All Buttoned Up Before." How he sets "puppy missing," and now, "Paradise Lost," he arrays a bride in "small caps," and a sonnet in "nonpareil," announces the languishing "live" in one sentence—transposes the world and develops the days that are few and evil in the next.

A poor jest ticks its way slowly into a printer's hand, like a clock just running down, and a strain of eloquence marches into the line, letter by letter. We fancy we can tell the difference by hearing by the ear, but perhaps not. The types that told a wedding yesterday announced a burial tomorrow—perhaps the same letters. They are the elements to make a world of—those types are a world with something in it as beautiful as spring, as rich as summer, and as grand as autumn flowers that frost cannot wilt—fruit that shall ripen for all time.

The newspaper has become the log-book of the age. It tells at what rate the world is running. We cannot find our "reckoning" without it.

True, the green grocer may bundle up a pound of candles in our last expressed thoughts, but it is only coming to base uses, something that is done times innumerable.

We console ourselves by thinking that ode can make that newspaper what he cannot make of living oaks—a bridge for time, that he can fling over the chasm of the dead years and walk safely back upon the shadowy sea into the far past. The singer shall not end his song, nor the soul be eloquent no more.

The realm of the press is enchanted ground. Sometimes the editor has the happiness of knowing that he has defended the right, exposed the wrong, protected the weak; that he has given utterance to a sentiment that has cheered somebody's solitary hour, made somebody happier, kindled a smile upon a sad face, or a hope in a heavy heart.

He may meet with that sentiment many years after; it may have lost all charms of its paternity, but he feels affection for it. He welcomes it as a long absent child. He reads it as for the first time, and wonders if indeed he wrote it for he has changed since then. Perhaps he could not give utterance to the sentiment now—perhaps he would not if he could.

It seems like the voice of his former self calling to his parents and there is something mournful in its tone. He begins to think—to remember why he wrote it, where his readers then and whither they had gone—what he was then and how much he has changed. So he muses, until he finds himself wondering if that thought of his will continue to float after he is dead, and whether he is really looking upon something that will survive him. And then comes the sweet consciousness that there is nothing in the sentence that he could wish unwritten—that it is a better part of him—a shred from a garment of immortality he shall leave behind him when he joins the "innumerable caravan," and takes his place in the silent hall of death.

Table of Contents

Acknowledgments v
Preface vi
"The Printer and His Types" viii

Chapter One - John's Early Life 1
Chapter Two - The War Years - 1861 3
Chapter Three - The War Years - 1862 18
Chapter Four - The War Years - 1863 32
Chapter Five - The War Years - 1864 46
Chapter Six - The War Years - 1865 56
Chapter Seven - After the War - Montana 61
Chapter Eight - Next Stop: California 69
Chapter Nine - On to Oregon 74
Chapter Ten - A Run for Public Office 91
Chapter Eleven - Spreading His Wings to *The Sun* 96
Chapter Twelve - Wending His Way to Retirement 105
Chapter Thirteen - Home At Last - Lorane 111

Epilogue 122
Addendum 126
Bibliography 136
Other Books by Pat Edwards

Chapter One

John's Early Life

When John O'Brien's family arrived in America in 1849, according to the 1920 U.S. Census, they settled in Connecticut—mainly in the Washington and New Haven areas. There was evidence that aunts, uncles and cousins made the journey, as well, but not necessarily all at the same time.

Some of John's family settled in the town of Washington, Connecticut early on, as it is listed as the birthplace of one of his step-sisters, Mary, who was born in 1850, and it was known that John attended private school there, but New Haven was considered home according to city directories. As a lad, John apprenticed at the J.H. Benham's Printer shop in New Haven, Connecticut where he studied under a "Mr. Gunn," and developed his interest in the trade of newspapers and printing.

An article featuring Captain John O'Brien, was published in 1892 by the San Francisco Typographical Union No. 21 newsletter called the *Pacific Union Printer*. It tells of John's early life quite eloquently.

John O'Brien was born on the 18th day of September, 1840, in County Leitrim, Ireland, coming to the Irishman's land of Promise with his parents when he was in his seventh year. The family found

This is believed to be the 4th Connecticut Volunteers which later became the 1st Connecticut Heavy Artillery regiment. In the background is the J.H. Benham Printers where John O'Brien apprenticed before enlisting in the Union army. *"Civil War Soldiers Assembly, New Haven" (2000.211.5) The Connecticut Historical Society*

a home in New Haven, Connecticut, struggling bravely for all that came to them in the new land, as so many Irish families have done, and the boy, John, was sent to school in Washington, Connecticut, for one summer and four winters. It was a brief schooling. It would have been too brief, perhaps, for any but a sharp witted Irish lad. But, John's possible earnings were needed by his family, and he was put in that wider school from which so many of the thought lenders of the land have graduated – a printing office.

At the breaking out of the war he was learning his trade in the printing office of John H. Benham, corner of Church and Chapel Streets, New Haven, and his ear, like so many men of foreign birth, was of the first to hear the call to arms in defense of the loved land. He was only an apprentice member of the New Haven Typographical Union then, but his allegiance has never swerved, and his connection with the organization has never for a day been severed...

Chapter Two

The War Years - 1861

When the rumblings of war became strong and the first shots were fired in April 1861, John became one of the first men in Connecticut to enlist as a private in Company F of the 4th Connecticut Volunteer Infantry, the first regiment mustered into the three-year service of the United States.

Referring back to the *Pacific Union Printer* article...

It proudly bore a silk banner made by the citizens of San Francisco, to be presented to the first regiment to be so mustered in. There are streamers attached to that flag today, and the names of eighteen battles are inscribed on it and in all of those battles, John O'Brien, who had enlisted as a private, participated.

At the time of his enlistment, he was described as 5' 7" in height with a dark complexion, grey eyes and dark brown hair and he listed his occupation as "printer."

He reported for duty in Hartford, Connecticut in May 1861.

John proved to be a prolific letter writer as he recorded his experiences throughout the war. One of his favorite correspondents was a young female cousin by the name of Mary Walker. Fortunately, Mary, who was only four years younger than John, had the foresight to save all of the letters she received from him, and these provide a rich look into the day-to-day activities of a Union soldier.

John O'Brien   His cousin, Mary Walker

The first of the letters that John wrote to Mary describe the conditions in camp those first few weeks. It was dated May 20, 1861 and sent from Hartford, Connecticut via his uncle, Thomas O'Brien.

Thomas has paid me a flying visit, and as he is going back to New Haven on his way to New York, I thought I would send you these few lines by him. We are camped out like those soldiers you saw in Peck's Lot, only we have tents built of wood instead of canvass. We expect to go into camp tomorrow in a place called the Babcock Farm, then we shall be situated exactly like them, have regular tents and get our victuals cooked in the camp and have it dealt out according to the army regulations.

Many of the men are sick and some of ours have been sick, owing, I think, to the locality in which we are placed. The ground is wet, and has pools of stagnant water in it. The straw which we filled our beds with was damp, and that alone ought to give us all colds, but I dried mine in the sun, and have sunned my bed every day until it was perfectly dry.

I am in good health and feel quite contented, for I have been away from home too much to get home-sick. I have been sentinel one day and several fellows tried to run by me, but they could not come it. One fellow tried to pull the gun out of my hand, but he was not quite smart enough. In the scuffle, he broke my watch chain, and my bayonet made a hole through his clothes and when it began to prick him, it fetched him to his senses. If I had reported him to the Capt. of the Guard he would have been kept under guard and fed on bread and water, but I didn't want to take advantage of him for he belonged to my company.

I think that we shall go to New Haven to embark for the seat of war, but it is uncertain, for some say we will have to go to New London, and learn the Artillery practice in Fort Trumbull, but I hope not for we are all anxious to go to Washington as soon as possible.

We have not got our clothes yet, but think we shall get them this week. If we do, I shall get my likeness taken, but when we shall get them it is uncertain. We think that we shall get paid off as soon as we go into camp and that is tomorrow, and perhaps we will get our clothes also, but that is uncertain like every thing else. I think, we may not go to Washington until near July, so that I shall have time to hear from you by letter at least... P.S. Direct your letters (to) me the care of Capt. Hollenback Box 1072 Hartford, Conn.

In John's second letter to Mary, dated May 31, 1861, he tells about the expectations he has for the near future...

I am entirely well, in every respect, only a little sick of Hartford. It is a miserable place for a camp. They keep us awful busy, something for us to do all the time so you must not expect a very long epistle this time... There is no telling what they will do with us yet. Rumor says we will leave here next Wednesday. I hope it is for New Haven, but it will probably be either to Statent (sp) Island or else to Washington.

In this same letter, John also reveals his good nature by telling Mary about a possible suitor.

I have had a letter from Bernard Brennan. He says he is coming to New Haven the fourth of July, when he expects to be made acquainted with Miss Mary Walker, and thinks he would like to gain her good will. He is on the lookout for his better half and I tell him he cannot find a better one than your self. He is a nice young man, and deserves a good girl, and he would know how to appreciate her services, in the journey of life, and place her in a respectable position, so that it would not be his fault if she was not happy.

He also revealed his concern for a cousin, probably Mary's brother, who was considering enlisting with the Confederate army...

I am glad to hear that William thinks of coming home and I hope for his own good, and Annie's sake, he will, for if he gets into the Southern Army he will see hardship.

As we progress through the letters, I won't have space to include much more than John's military commentary, but he always wrote with courtesy, humor and respect when addressing personal and family matters in his correspondence with Mary.

A long silence passed before Mary received John's next letter, dated September 23, 1861 and postmarked from Camp Lyons in Montgomery County, Maryland.

I suppose New Haven must be rather a lonesome place, for it must have taken a large number of young men from there to fill all those companies that have been organized there since I left, and as far as I can learn, business is so dull that they could not stay there if they had not gone to the war.

According to Mary's great-great grandson, John Dwyer, "As he rose in rank so did his expression of patriotism. He began to lose patience with those who stayed at home feeling that they increased the burden for those who served and that lack of manpower extended the war."

I have never been sorry that I came, yet a soldier's life is harder than I would choose, and no one need envy their lot, and when this rebellion is put down they will all be glad to lay down the sword and musket and go back to the workshop. Some of us may come home with a pair of wooden legs, or might do things that would be more patriotic – leave their bodies on a victorious and well fought field – and their graves would always be a warning to those who seek to overthrow one of the best governments that has ever been formed by the hand of man. Yet most of us will come back again and I have no doubt but that New Haven will soon be as busy as it was a year ago and all those absent ones will be back again to make the now desolate homes happy.

I have been in the service nearly five months. It is over four since we were sworn in and it is only a few days since we were paid. We were paid for three months and nine days. Each man received $37.98, so now we will have lively times as long as the money lasts. The only drawback to spending it is that we are not near a city or a large town now. We buy what we need of sutlers[1] and they charge nearly double the real value of an article. When we left Hartford, our first stopping place was in Chambersburg Pa. We only stayed there a few days, and from there we went to Hagerstown, Md. We went all this distance by railroad. We stayed in Hagerstown for nearly ten weeks. We were there when our division was in the battle of Porters Field and Falling Water(s)[2], but we were guarding the town then and (I) did not go. The first battle was fought within nine miles of us and after the fight, I went to see the field. Our troops drove the enemy to Martinsburgh. This happened about the first of July. We all went one time five miles expecting that Gen. Johnston was crossing the river, and waited for him there all day but he did not try it, and at night we went back to camp again.

I went to Harper's Ferry once. Soon after that Johnston went to Manassas Gap and helped Bouregard at the battle of Bulls Run, and he never troubled the upper Potomac after that so we have had no alarms since and I have been in the field over four months and have not smelled powder yet.

We left Hagerstown about five weeks ago, and went to Frederick City, Md. We stayed there three weeks and are now in Montgomery County, twenty-two miles from Washington, D.C. and within twelve miles of Chain Bridge, three miles from the Potomac, and one mile from Darnestown. We are encamped close to Gen. Banks' headquarters. We expect new clothes in a few days. We are going to have the regular U.S. uniform – that is, blue clothes.

John shows that his location at the time was with the Banks Division via Washington, D.C.

At about this time, John heard the news that his father, William J. O'Brien, had also re-enlisted in the Union army as part of the 6th Connecticut Volunteers.

Many forts were being set up around Washington, D.C. to protect our nation's capital in case of attack. It was the

---

[1] sutler: a civilian provisioner to an army post often with a shop on the post

[2] http://battleoffallingwaters.com/battleinfo.html

assignment of the 4th Connecticut Volunteers and other units to help build these fortifications for that purpose.

In his next letter, dated October 2, 1861, and mailed from Camp Ingalls in Virginia, John tells of the work being done on those forts...

We are building two forts and they are about three miles from Washington and where we can have a good view of the city. I expect that we will stay here all winter – if so, it will be fortunate for us although our labor may be severe (it) will not be subject to the extreme hardship of those who are on the outposts of the army. There is nothing so tiresome as marching and lying under arms waiting for orders, etc. The weather is stormy and we have very cool nights. It seems as if we have colder weather than it is in New Haven, but I suppose it is owing to our outdoor life. The country, where free from woods, is covered with tents and on every hill is a fort. There is a dozen in sight of ours. Fort Corcoran is situated two miles and a half north of us I went to see it a few days ago, It is the largest fort in the vicinity of Washington (D.C.), and it speaks well for the patriotism of the 89th Regt. who built it.

Before war broke out, this country was nearly all covered with woods, but since it has come into the possession of the U.S. troops, the timber has all been cut down and the trees (are) lying on the ground, and it would be impossible for an army to march over them, and if the South should try to take Washington, they would have to march on roads that would lead them through several forts.

A letter that is missing its front page and the date seems to be the next one in progression since John still shows a return address of Washington, D.C. It is assumed that it was written in the early part of November 1861. He talks about the fact that there is a lot of illness running through the company and that out of 101 men that came with Company F, only 60 are "fit for duty."

We have only six tents to a company. When we left Hartford we had thirteen, so we have to pack ourselves rather close in them – too close for health and comfort. When the weather was pleasant I slept out in the open air, but now, we have very cool nights, and a good deal of wet weather which compels me to sleep in a tent. But it is not as unhealthy sleeping in such close quarters now as it was a month ago.

We have to carry all our housekeeping arrangements in our knapsacks. Our bed consists of a woolen blanket, one India rubber blanket and an overcoat... We place the India rubber blanket on the ground then wrap ourselves in our woolen blanket and put our overcoat on top of us. The first thing I do after I get up in the morning is to fold up my bed and put it in my knapsack. When the sun shines, I take all my clothes and air them a couple hours so as to have a dry bed I always take my clothes off the same as if I was at home, only keeping my underclothes on, and always put them in the rubber blanket, and there with my spare shirt I put under me. I have six yards of brown drilling which I put on top of them for a sheet. It is light and only weighs about a pound. This makes a comfortable bed using my woolen blanket and overcoat to cover me. I sleep sound all night – never wake up until morning. Some of the boys never undress themselves or even take off their shoes. They have as many things as I but now they tell me they are almost froze every night. We expect new clothes every day. We wear the same clothes now that we wore in Hartford and some of them are as ragged as they could be.

Apparently done with fort building for the time, John tells about having to drill eight hours a day and the rest of their time is taken up with cleaning equipment and washing their own clothes and dishes.

You asked me if I was not getting sick of a soldier's life. I never felt as though I should like it and it was always the best of my ambition to be either a soldier or a fireman, but I should regard it a misfortune to be a man and be ignorant of the art of war and to tell the truth, I am getting so that I like it. It is not much duller in New Haven, then it is with us just now. There is no alarms or skirmishing going on now. I have not heard a cannon for the past week.

Fort Richardson November 22, 1861...

Dear Cousin Mary... Providence has kindly favored me, for thus far in my Campaign experience I have not seen an unwell moment – life and good health are the two greatest blessing(s) which is given us and for those gifts I have much reason to be thankful.

The war seems a long way away during this period. John's letters turn to talking about family and teasing Mary about her social life. He's now at Fort Richardson, Virginia which is where he will spend most of his time during the war. He does take time to share some news...

I have sent a letter to Father – he is now at Hilton Head, South Carolina, and is in good health.

He also tells of life at camp...

My old friends in Washington (not my aunts) have been so good as to send to your young man a barrel of all kinds of good things. I was one of the four happy recipients. They sent a half barrel of all kinds of eatables – cakes, several kinds of preserves, catsup, etc. and a half barrel of clothes – 40 pair of stockings, shirts, handkerchiefs, towels, etc. I had among other things a cheese – this is all I have left of the eatables, but the other things will last all winter. We have fires in our tents. the weather is as warm as I could expect, but it is bad being on guard. I have to be on guard once a week – 24 hours.

John took out time to visit a bit of history, too.

I have been to the city of Alexandria, and went to the Marshall House where Elsworth (sp) was shot. I went all through the building and cut a piece of wood from the floor where he fell. There is a large hole cut in the floor, and the stairs is all cut up and taken away. It was a small place, not large enough to hold a dozen men – the passage way, that is. It was an ugly roof to go out in, being very high and steep – the rooms are all full of names. I am going to send you a small piece of the wood, for I suppose some of your friends would like to see it.

The event of which John was describing in the letter above related to Elmer Ephraim Ellsworth (1837-1861) who was the first Union officer killed in the American Civil War. He died while removing a Confederate flag from the roof of the Marshall House Inn of Alexandria, Virginia, at the behest of Abraham Lincoln, who was a close personal friend. President Lincoln wanted it removed because the flag had, at that time, been visible from the White House and was considered a defiant sign of the Confederacy.

The next letter that Mary received from John was dated December 5, 1861. During the interim, John was one of 12 men selected out of Company F to begin training with the large cannons. The same number of men were chosen from each company and would eventually form Company F of the 1st Connecticut Heavy Artillery Regiment *serving under General McClellan in the Army of the Potomac,* according to a 1930 article in the *Oregon Labor Press.*

There are twelve men selected out of six companies in the regiment to be artillery men – we practice 4 hours daily on those guns . They are so large that they will throw balls weighing 32 pounds out sight – that is we cannot see the ground where they would strike. We have a rifled cannon on which I drill that will hit a tree four miles aft. I have got to be quite expert, and when they have visitors, I am called upon to help work the guns.

We expect that we will have an artillery uniform before long. The rest of the Regt. drills two hours in the morning, but they will not be artillery men unless some of us should get shot or promoted which is not likely to happen more especially to myself.

I don't think there is any likelihood of my going home until our three years are up for they are going to consolidate the army sometime before Congress adjourns, and if they should, we would be as likely to stay three years as any regt. in the field.

We were reviewed by a member of Gen. McClellan's staff days ago and he says he has not seen so good a Regt. in the field. We receive much praise and if we are as good as represented will be kept as long as needed.

At the defenses of Washington, at Yorktown on the Peninsular and at City Point and Petersburg, the First Connecticut Heavies were a favorite subject of the notable photographers of the era. Some of the most memorable and famous wartime images are of these men, their camps and of their equipment. John Dwyer

Military Map of N.E. Virginia Showing Forts and Roads

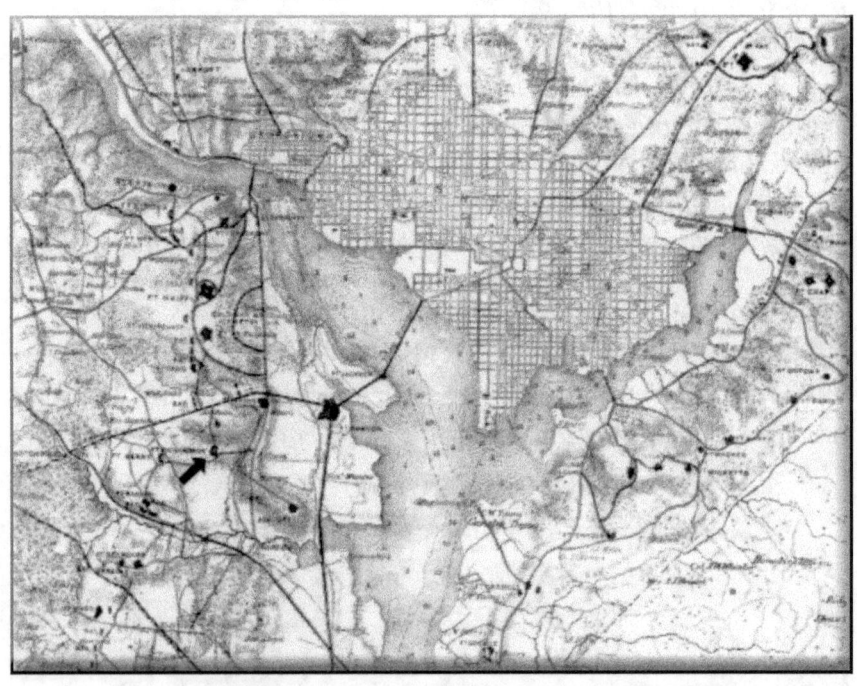

The black arrow indicates where Ft. Richardson was located in the area around Washington, D.C. (*Library of Congress*)

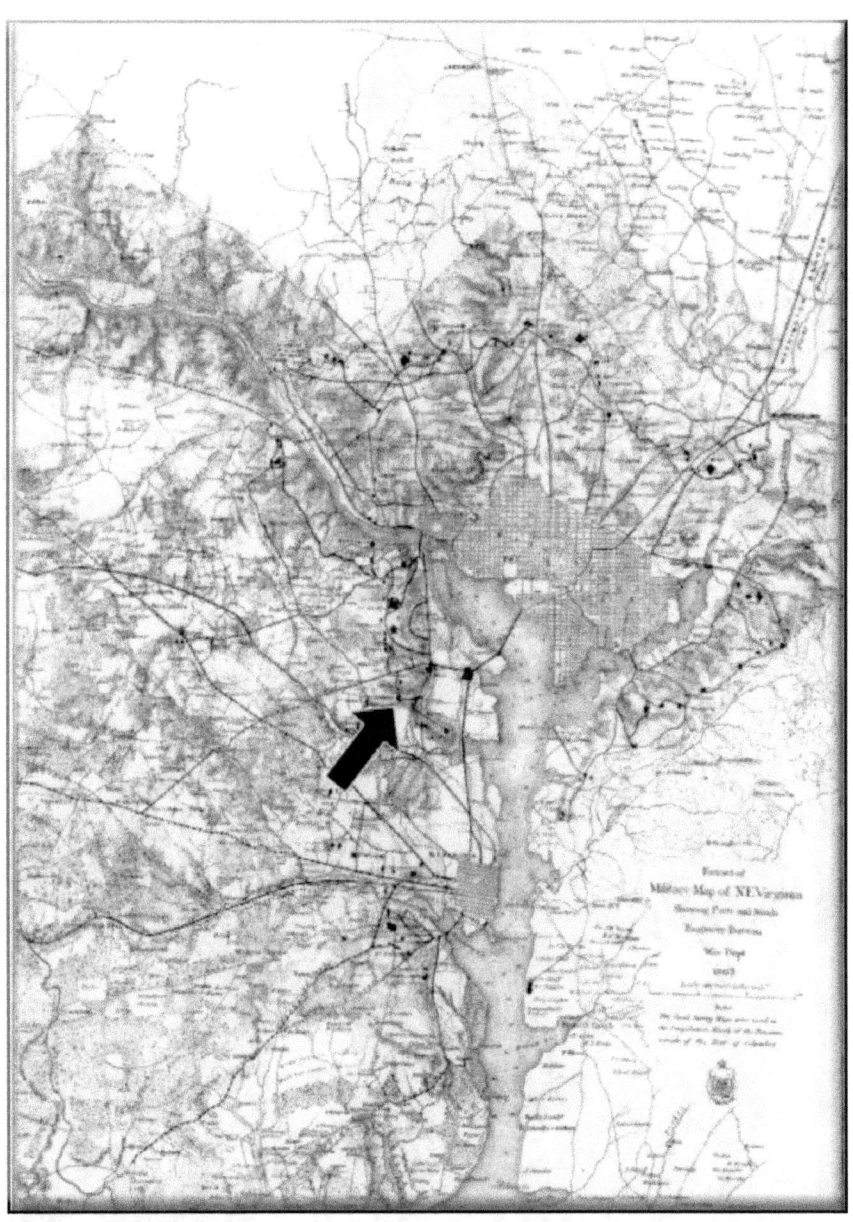

Courtesy of the United States. War Department. Engineer Bureau. (*Library of Congress*)

The 1st Connecticut Heavy Artillery under the command of Colonel Tyler at Fort Richardson - 1861 (*Wikimedia*)

First Regiment Connecticut Heavy Artillery - ~1861 (*Library of Congress*)

A soldier stands watch at a church between battles at Bull Run - 1862 (*Wikimedia*)

Union troops awaiting the train transport. Manassus Junction, Virginia. Battle of Bull Run. 1862 (*Library of Congress*)

Union soldiers manning the defenses of Washington, D.C. (*Wikimedia*)

John's cousin, Mary Walker

John's half-brother, William F. O'Brien (b. 1846) studied at St. Mary's Catholic Seminary, Baltimore MD after the war. He returned to Connecticut and served at St. John's Church in the town of Middletown.

Chapter Three

The War Years - 1862

It was suddenly the year, 1862, and shortly after, on January 4, 1862, Mary Walker received a letter from John with New Years greetings and thank yous for cakes and the gift she had sent him for Christmas.

There wasn't a lot of time to celebrate the holidays, because the regiment got word that Governor Francis Harrison Pierpont of the restored government in Virginia was going to appear to review the troops.

The Governor was here to review us the Friday after Christmas, and it took several days to get ready for it. He was going to be here Monday before New Years Day to review us also but did not come, much to the disappointment of all... I had to go help trim the barracks in the fort for his reception, for the officers were going to give him a supper and laid out $300 for it. They were fixed up in good shape — it took two days to trim it in evergreen. They were lit up with Chinese lanterns, some of them were gaudy enough to suit any body.

John's mood seems to be light and he appears to be settling in well as a soldier despite the cold winter.

Sunday Jan 5th — I had not time enough to finish this letter last evening so I have to put it off until tonight. Last night was very cold, and also today, and tonight is the coldest night we have had yet. We have a fire in our tent and we are supplied with plenty of blankets so that we do not mind it much more than you in your warm buildings in New Haven. Every thing seems to go on smoothly with us and we have had a very happy time throughout the holidays.

Mary received her second letter of the year from John on January 30, 1862. He was still at Fort Richardson, Virginia.

We have some very stormy weather now-a-days — to-day for one has given us it share of mud and water. I tell you this mud is a delightful thing. Just step outside the tent and our shoes are all covered with it. Our tent floor will get some of it. Where there are sixteen of us going in and out all day, it will not be long before we have a carpet soft and as nice as you please. but not very agreeable as you may easily imagine. Once in a while a fellow will upset a cup of coffee and this only adds another charm to such a covering for our floor. When night comes we have to spread our blankets in this mud it is not so very nice, but there is no getting away from it. The thing must be done. Some say the mud is all that saves the "Secesh" from an advance of our army — being too muddy to transport provisions and munitions of war. They may like mud and be thankfull for it too — perhaps pray for it — but give us pleasant weather for a change. I believe there was two weeks of stormy weather so much so that we did not see the sun during that time and I believe that the next two will follow suit — as the boys say when playing eucher — but I hope not. I expect you will find some of the Virginia mud on this sheet you will not have to put glasses on to find it either.

In this letter, John seemed very excited to get the new trimmings for his cap and uniform. Up until this point, he wore the blue trimmings of the infantry with a bugle on his cap. Now that he was an artillery man with Company F of the 1st Connecticut Heavy Artillery Regiment, he was to wear scarlet trimmings with two crossed cannons on his cap. In this way it was easy to tell one regiment from another. For the mounted cavalry, the insignia worn on the cap was crossed swords.

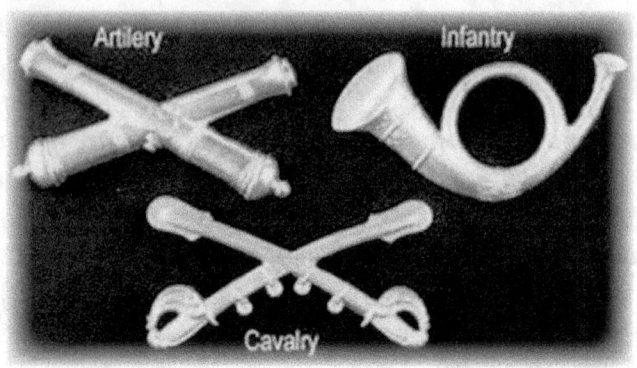

We are to have about a thousand more men added to this regiment and are to have nearly twice as many officers when the regiment is full – how soon, it will be hard to tell for I think it is not very easy to get men to go a soldering now, but I understand a few must go if they have to draft to get them, and MR. LINCOLN may have to leave his young son and go to the wars – that he may have some stories to tell him by-and-by to keep him good-natured when he gets big enough to exercise the privilege of free speech. If he is not armed with war stories, he will make music – perhaps he may hear some tall sqaling.

The letter that John sent Mary on February 12 from Fort Richardson, gives us some insight into his future devotion to the organization of trade unions.

I am glad to hear that JOHNSTON has found a good place to finish learning his trade – it is the best thing he could do to serve that length of time. He will be a better workman for it.

But, for now, John is very much involved in a war that seems to be taking more time than expected. He's not in the midst of battle yet, but there is news to be had on the front.

We have glorious news from Gen. Burnside's command. We hear of the capture of Roanoke and the burning of Elizabeth City.

...We have had some very pleasant days lately and the mud is getting dried up, and if this weather holds out long we shall have an advance. I learn that regiments around us keep their knapsacks packed ready to go at a moment's notice. How soon the war will be over no one knows and in all probability we will stay three years.

You need not feel at all unconcerned about your manuscript, for it is very good, if it was bad I would be able to make it out for I am used to reading all kinds of writing. I think you must be sorely puzzled to make out these letters of mine, for I believe I could print one in good shape but writing is almost out of my line of business.

Fort Richardson, Virginia, February 27, 1862

I received a letter from you the 19th, also three papers all of which I am thankful for and I hope I will someday be able to return your kindness, for it is worth remembering, although it is a trifling token of friendship to be so remembered, but a person's friends do not always think it worth their while to send a paper and seem to forget that there is a daily mail to our camp and if it was not for some enterprising newsboys, we would be without news. When we first came here it was very hard to get papers but now we have several regular newspaper men. I tell you this lest you would think we are entirely destitute of news matter. (Spoken like the newsman he will eventually become...)

With this letter, it appears that the war is gaining momentum and there seems to be a new tone of excitement in John's letter.

Tomorrow is a general muster day. The Col. calls the muster roll, and afterwards, the rolls are signed and we shall get paid in about two weeks, The State owes us $10, and should have paid us a month ago. We cannot get to Alexandria now so easily as we could when we first came – only four enlisted men get a pass, so you see we are kept in camp very close. I had a pass on the 17th inst, but it rained and could not use it.

Every regiment around us are under marching order and very soon all the troops will move. We have good drying weather, and the ground begins to look natural. It has been so muddy that it was almost unbearable. Spring will soon come, for it is now almost March and the Spring is some two or three weeks earlier here. We think we have past a dreary winter. All are anxious for a forward movement. Everywhere the marching orders were received with cheers and every demonstrations of joy for they think the sooner we take Manassas, the soon we get through.

A month passes before John's next letter arrives and it brings with it more news...

I never have been busier in my life I was detailed to drill recruits, and when not doing that I had to study **Hardee's Tactics** *that I might be asked to do it right so that all my time has been employed. I have to go* *on guard in turn besides. I had a pass to Washington one day last week. I had 24 hours so that I had time to see the city.*

We are under marching orders and shall leave here in a few days. Where we are going I don't know, but I guess that we are going far south... The recruits are unhealthy, but the veterans are all in good health. Two of the recruits have died and some more are very sick.

In the previous letter, John refers to his study of *Hardee's Tactics*. This was a collection of tactical information put together by William Joseph Hardee (1815–1873). He was a career U.S. Army officer, serving during the Second Seminole War and in the Mexican-American War. Apparently, he was captured and held prisoner in the last war until he was released as a POW in an exchange agreement.

During the American Civil War, he sided with the South and became a general. Hardee served in the Western Theater — in the Atlanta Campaign of 1864 and the Carolinas Campaign of 1865 — where he surrendered with General Joseph E. Johnston to Sherman in April 1865. Hardee's writings about military tactics were widely used on both sides in the conflict.

According to Mary's great-great grandson, John Dwyer, "John O'Brien took seriously the science of war. He studied much and was recognized" for his knowledge.

It was another month before Mary heard from John again. The next letter was written on April 20, 1862 from Camp Ingalls near Yorktown, Virginia. John gives some details as they prepare for action...

Since I last wrote we have changed our habitation and are now close to Yorktown, near Fortress Monroe. We left Fort Richardson on the 2nd inst. We landed at Shipping Point the 10th inst. and when we unloaded our siege train we came within 8 miles of Yorktown where we are now. In a few days we shall be ready, and when we get all our guns mounted we expect to give them fits, for we have the best of cannon and any quantity of ammunition.

But, first, he had to get over a bout a measles that he picked up at Fort Monroe. While he was trying to recoup from the measles, he was notified of a welcome promotion...

...(I) *am now the 9th corporal in an artillery company. We have 8 sergeants and 12 corporals, and 150 men.*

There was no time for celebrating a promotion or nursing an illness however...

We are busier now than ever before. We were working all night loading guns and taking them near Yorktown where we have been throwing up fortifications. We have got six 18 inch mortars to work and when they have thrown up sufficient earthwork to protect us, we will be at work. The Rebels are trying to get our range but do not succeed very well — no drums are allowed to be beaten, They send random shots very near us. The boys watch to see where they strike, dig them up and carry them into camp as trophies. It rained very hard all night and we are completely wet through. All the boys are sleeping while I am writing. I don't mind one night, but two nights generally makes me very sleepy. I don't believe we shall be called out again until nearly noon. We do not stop for Sunday in such times as these.

Almost another month passes before a letter arrives. This one is dated May 11, 1862 and he is still positioned near Yorktown.

I received your letter in due time but owing to so much hard work in getting our 18 inch mortars in position, and having to work both day and night, I have not felt much like writing during the past week. We had everything ready on Saturday the 3rd and on Sunday the 4th inst., they left Yorktown, which saved us one or two days of bombardment. Last Sunday we rested from our labors for the first time since we left Fort Richardson, and today also we have another rest — all of that sort of thing we know how to appreciate. We drill on the mortars twice on each weekday from 7 to 9 in morning and from 1 to 4 in the afternoon so you can see this leaves us very little time to clean equipments, cook slap-jacks, etc.

Our mortars are good playthings. (They) only weigh 18,000 pounds. The weather during the past week has been delightful. We are encamped close to a river (Wormsley's Creek) and it is as full of eels as they can live. I make a bob and catch in a few minutes enough for my dinner, and find them quite a luxury when a person has nothing but salt-horse as (we) *call it, known east as salt beef and hard bread and it is dreadful hard too. I mean to get some eels for dinner by and by too. It is necessary that I should have something good to eat Sunday's as well as other days. We pay 40 cents* per doz. for eggs and the same for butter and cheese per pound. Every man has a cubboard which he carries with him — we call it a haversack. Mine held 8 quarts of Secession flour which with other things I confiscated on last Sunday so you can judge how much it holds.

Yorktown is an old place and is composed of ancient buildings. The house where Washington and Cornwallis signed the terms of capitulation and where Lord Cornwallis surrendered his sword to Washington is below Yorktown close by our battery.

A hard lesson is learned for those who were not aware of the damage that land mines could do...

The rebels throw shot and shell every day we were to work on our batteries. Our camp is in sight of our parallels and early on Sunday morning we saw the men who were to work on them standing on the works. We began to suspect what happened. One went to see. We came very near getting blown up with concealed shells for we (had) no idea of such a thing until we saw a horse and rider blown to pieces. After that we looked out for them.

I shall have to close this epistle and by next July I will be where I can tell you about what I have seen.

May 31, 1862 brought the following news in an exceptionally short letter to Mary...

I was in a battle on Tuesday at or near Hanover. We are in the field as infantry and shall be in the fight at Richmond. There was a battle there this afternoon. The firing was awful. We have marched over 100 miles this week. I have no time to write any (more). Goodbye for the present.

Mary didn't hear from John until a letter dated June 21, 1862, arrived from a camp near New Bridge, Virginia, six miles from Richmond. After learning that Mary was traveling in the West, it brought back memories of his last trip to Detroit before the war, in 1856.

I almost wish I was a free man again so that I could travel, for there is nothing under the sun that would please me better and as soon as this War is over I shall go and see the world somewhere. I am afraid that that day is not near for it seems to hold out beyond all expectation.

The war becomes really personal for John...

One young German by the name of Henry Matts was killed yesterday while asleep in his tent. The rebels have planted a battery about a mile and a half from us of two 32 pounders (rifled) and have been throwing shot and shell at us all day. Several shell struck in our camp, but we did not apprehend any danger untill that unfortunate occurrence I have just mentioned. Young Matts left an aged mother in Germany and no doubt she thinks of the son who sends her part of his wages and wonders if all is well with him and prays for him and thinks as she finishes her hard day's labor and takes off her wooden shoes and sits in her straight-back chair that her boy may get rich away off in America and take care of her in her old age and that the world will not always think of her so roughly. But her boy is dead and already the epistle in which is wrote the sad tidings is on its way to Germany. Matts was beloved and respected by all his companions. He belonged to Co. I and was orderly to the Colonel.

We have been on several tramps about the country since I last wrote, but have not met the enemy yet. Where our boys go on picket they sometimes are so near the rebels pickets as to speak to them, but now they fire at one another so that they keep a greater distance and do not expose themselves. Our siege train is on its way home and before long we shall be blazing away at them again with great guns. The weather is very warm and we still have a good many rainy days. It will soon be the 4th of July – our second "fourth" in the army.

The summer passes and the next letter in Mary's collection was written on September 26, 1862 and sent from Fort Worth, Virginia, near Alexandria. John has been back from the Peninsular Campaign[1] for 6 weeks...

I have been in the ordnance department in Alexandria until about a week since. While there I had a very easy time, but the stores were all distributed and so the boats on which they were stored were discharged and myself sent back to my company. I am on guard today and it is a splendid day. I think how pleasant it would be if this thing was settled so that we might have a chance for some recreation, but as it is, we have got to do our duty and hope for the best.

---

[1] The Peninsula or Peninsular Campaign of the American Civil War was a major Union operation launched in southeastern Virginia from March through July 1862. It was the first large-scale offensive in that area of the war, referred to as the Eastern Theater.

John mentions in this letter that after leaving Richmond, he had one day off and he was able to check in with some of the other regiments in the area, visiting friends and most notably, his Uncle Thomas who was also serving.

Being absent without leave was not an option for him...

We have four drills every day and if a person is absent from one without leave he is tied up in the "spread eagle" style so you can easily imagine why I cannot have time to myself and to visit. I don't mean to complain, but my friends in New Haven thought it was strange that I did not go and see Uncle Tom and some others sooner.

John's letter of October 11, 1862 is mostly a relaxed, friendly letter in which he teases Mary about a mutual friend, but towards the end, he turns to some introspection about the war and his service...

I certainly have reason to be thankful for God's goodness to me in preserving me from all the dangers incidental to war and I trust the day is not far distant when this strife will be over and all who are now in the field will be restored to their friends, but I apprehend that many will fall yet before the war is ended.

Another year is coming to a close and in John's next letter dated November 16, 1862 from Fort Worth, Virginia, he focuses on the discipline expected of and enforced on soldiers during this time. The subject came up when Mary asked him again when he was going to have a picture taken to send to her. It's one of his longest letters and I'm going to include it almost in its entirety, because I believe that it gives a good indication of what kind of man John O'Brien was...

I tried the best way possible to get to the city of Alexandria but could not prevail on my officers to give me a pass. I waited awhile and then tried again and in about a week hence I shall try once more and then if nothing happens to disappoint me I will send you one at any rate. You shall have one as soon as possible. I don't like to trouble the officers for a pass too often. They are limited to give only one pass each day and they have to be sent to headquarters to be countersigned. I am kept very close to camp and sometimes it is very difficult to get away to go any distance. It is of no account how well a soldier has behaved if he is caught doing wrong once there is nothing he has done can atone for it and if a non-commissioned officer is caught disobeying orders, his punishment is more severe than if he was a private for they will reduce him to the ranks.

When I was on the Peninsular I was put under arrest for not reporting a man who took off his equipments while on duty as a sentinel. If I had reported this fellow he would have been placed under charge of a guard for over two months and lost his pay and allowance. I was released next day, but I have known non-commissioned officers broke for things similar to that. If it was not for being kept so strict I suppose I could go to Alexandria without a pass. Two of our officers are now under arrest for absenting themselves from duty without leave and I think they will be either cashiered or fined heavily. I tell you this to give you some idea of how we are governed here by officers. They are as tyrannical as they can be for they can do with us as they please, but a campaign like what we went through last summer takes the wind out of their sails nicely. They are not to blame for what they do, for it is very hard to govern a company of men for some are "hard cases" and if they were to have their own way, in a short time there would be no army.

You must not think that we have a hard life to live from what I have said – it is only hard if we have a mind to make it so. Today we had inspection and review. We had to go to Ft. Ward. The whole regiment was there. We have not been together since we were on the Peninsular until today. We are having the best times now that we have enjoyed since we came out. Our quarters are admirable for soldiers.

We have to drill twice a day – an artillery drill in the morning of an hour's duration and an infantry drill in the bayonet exercise in the afternoon of an hour and a half. Once a week we have a battalion drill which lasts full half a day.

In your last you expressed a wish that I would be spared to come home. I am sure there is no one looking with more pleasure to the time when we shall be mustered out of the service than myself, but I am afraid it will not be until we have served our time out.

The army of the Potomac have now lost their chief, General McClellan, a man whom the army almost idolized. I know and believe there is no officer who can do what he has done. I have seen him cheered by men who had fought for one week – men who were scarcely able to *say a word — cheer him. If they did not have confidence in him they would not have shown him such favors and if he was not worthy of their confidence he would not have been so much esteemed. I am sorry to think he has been relieved from his command. I believe the war will last a long time and if I ever again see the city of New Haven, it will be when I am one year and six months older.*

For those unfamiliar with what happened, General George McClellan, was a controversial figure when he was relieved of his command by President Abraham Lincoln in November 1862. He was obviously idolized by many who served under him, but others in command thought differently.

McClellan was known to be a perfectionist when it came to battle planning and preparation. He was deliberate and thorough when he had the time to study the circumstances, but when it came to making split-second decisions on the battlefield, itself, he was criticized for being too conservative in his assessments when offensive moves were needed.

President Abraham Lincoln lost trust in his general-in-chief when he overestimated the Confederate strength in several battles, backing off when he could have gone on the offensive. The Battle of Antietam sealed his fate when he allowed Lee's army to retreat after the Battle of Antietam, instead of showing the strength needed to make it a decisive victory.

It was after that battle that McClellan was relieved of his command by President Lincoln.

John's letter continued...

I am glad you are enjoying yourself so well and that you like your young friend of whom you made mention and am also glad that Thomas is at home for more than one reason and hope that he will never think of enlisting. You need never trouble yourself but what your letters are interesting, for I assure you they are prizes to a soldier and a friend who has your best welfare at heart.

John brings the year to a close with a letter dated December 13, 1862. In it he delivers the welcome news to Mary that he has finally been able to get his picture taken. In this letter, he playfully puts himself in the third person to tell Mary about the experience of sitting for the photo.

I had a great deal of trouble in bringing the original (himself) *into a calm state of feeling for it was so long since he saw a camera that he mistook it for a battery in the hands of an enemy and when the artist* (the photographer) *turned the instrument on him I was afraid he would not stand fire. The skirmish lasted only a few seconds when the artist by a skillful manoeuver withdrew his forces and left our hero in possession of the field. The victory was complete and as our hero was the only man left, I succeeded in sending you his daguerreotype which I had taken on the spot and now hope he will have a chance to rest with his laurels. I think it will be many days before love of country will ever induce him to try it over.*

Only a small, sobering part of the letter dealt with the war...

Two companies of our regiment went with their batteries to Fredericksbourgh and were to the bombardment of that place. A batch of recruits for this regt. are now at headquarters.

Union battery with 13-inch (330 mm) seacoast mortars, Model 1861, during siege of Yorktown, Virginia during the Peninsula Campaign. 1862 (*Library of Congress*)

The aftermath. Soldiers survey the ruin of Richmond, KY 1862.
(*Library of Congress*)

President Abraham Lincoln and Gen. George B. McClellan at a military encampment at Antietam; 1862 (*Library of Congress*)

Colonel Tyler reads a dispatch at Ft. Richardson; 1862 (*Library of Congress*)

Chapter Four

The War Years - 1863

The year, 1863, was a very important one as far as the American Civil War was concerned. On January 1, 1863, the terms of President Abraham Lincoln's Emancipation Proclamation were set in motion. It freed all black Americans who had been enslaved.

With the proclamation, the numbers of blacks enlisting in the Union army increased and all-black regiments were formed. By the end of the war, over 200,000 black troops had enlisted in the Union cause.

John O'Brien's first letter of 1863, dated January 4, was mainly an easy-going one, teasing Mary about taking some of his past "joking foolishness" for "sober earnestness." It did turn serious, however, in reply to Mary's concern that an acquaintance of hers in New Haven, a Lieut. Mitchell, had died in battle. John made the comment, *I know that many people in West Haven have lost friends. There has been a hard battle fought out west at Murfreesboro – it is said to be one of the bloodiest yet fought.*

John continued his narrative on Lieut. Mitchell in his next letter, dated January 22, 1863.

I think you said Lieut. Mitchell belonged to the 51st N.Y. I have been on long marches with the 5th. If he belongs to that regt. he can be proud of it. I never remember of seeing the 51st. I think the 51st was in Hookers Division, but am not certain if it was...

We are not in so much danger as infantry for an infantry man is more afraid of balls than bullets. But the latter kills more than the former. I am afraid you will see another New Year's Day before you see our regt. marching up Chapel Street.

John's letter of February 9, 1863, became more focused on the war and his predictions for it.

We still belong to the "Army of the Potomac" but there is no danger of an advance within a month at least and possibly not until April. Most of our regt. is doing garrison duty in front of the Capital and we will have to be relieved from that duty before there will be a chance for us to go into a battle, so that you need not have any fears. But if we leave the fort where we are now, I hope it will be to the "front." We have everything here to our liking — good quarters which were built at our own expense and if we have to leave them, we must take to tent life again. It does not make much difference as to the place, for it would be more disagreeable within sight of the Capitol building than it would within hearing of the bells of Richmond if anything.

There is one consolation in being in the 1st Conn. and that is that we have only one more summer to serve and then our time will be drawing to a close. I do not think the war will end in the next three years. I believe there will have to be a very large draft every year while it lasts so that there are plenty of men left yet in New Haven and the state that now have no idea of being soldiers who will fall victims to the rebellion. No bounty — no matter how large — will ever induce men to re-enlist so that when the sun sets on the 22nd of May in the year of 1864, it will set on this regt. for the last time, unregretted by no one of my companions. Whatever glory we shall have gained will live in history — but those (the greater part) who have gained it will be left as mementoes of the war in unknown graves in the land of chivalry...

P.S. I have heard our new Chaplain preach. I have heard a great many sermons, but he delivered one on "Love of Country" and I think it was as (good) as any I ever heard. He has the appearance of a good man and hope he will accomplish much good among us.

Another milestone was reached in the annals of the Civil War when on March 3, 1863, President Lincoln and Congress issued the First Conscription Act. At that time, men who were between the ages of 20-45 were considered draft-eligible. The First Conscription Act, however, provided the ability for draft-eligible men to pay $300 for an exemption or have someone paid to substitute for him in battle.

By the time that John O'Brien writes his next letter to Mary, dated March 4, 1863, he has returned to Fort Richardson, Virginia from Fort Worth where he had been stationed for many months.

We have plenty of work to do since we came here but have our houses moved and rebuilt so that we are quite comfortable. We are now clearing up ground for a new parade ground so that we are at our old business again – that is digging stump. I saw an old friend of mine from Washington, Connecticut a few days since and from him I learned all that was going on in those regions. I was glad to see a person who I knew so near from home – a thing which does not happen very often.

I have just received a letter from Father. He is at Hilton Head and is enjoying good health.

I am on guard today or else I would be very brief and, as it is, I think I shall have to be because I have not much news. I have been to a regular church but once since I left Hagerstown. This may surprise you some, but a soldier's Sunday does not amount to much. We are generally reviewed and inspected on Sunday, unless it rains, then we have it to ourselves.

In the same letter, John comments on the upcoming Connecticut gubernatorial election between a "Copperhead" candidate, Thomas Hart Seymour, and William Alfred Buckingham.

The term "Copperhead" used in the 1860s refers to a vocal faction of Democrats in the northern part of the United States who opposed the American Civil War. They wanted an immediate peace settlement with the Confederates.

I suppose there is a great deal of excitement in New Haven about the coming election. Our Regiment could not vote the copperhead ticket under any circumstances, but Buckingham is not our favorite. I hope that we will have some sensible man, but that is impossible for the next year.

The next letter from Fort Richardson was dated March 31, 1863. Upon learning that Mary was taking up the trade of dressmaking, John had mixed feelings about it—one of which would impact him in later years and another statement that he would eventually reverse.

I first thought on commencing to read your last letter that you were soon about to become the wife of some lucky young man — an event which I would much rather have happen than the one you speak of. But I think that if you can make a change for the better, you had better embrace the first opportunity to do so. If the trade of a dressmaker is more suitable to your taste than any other trade, why, then of course, you will be in your appropriate sphere in following that avocation. The trades are much better for men than to be without them, for if you have one you can depend on it and if it becomes necessary to follow some other business and in it you should fail, why then in an emergency you can always fall back on your old occupation.

If I had my life to live over again I would never learn a trade. I always had a desire to get a good education. It may not be too late yet, but still I might have had it now if I had done better. I know that if I had one, it would be of great advantage in the Army. A man who has a college education is sure of commission. If I had a commission, I would follow the profession of a soldier during my lifetime, but I never could be induced to enlist again unless it would be for a very short time in case of great danger.

April 27, 1863, Fort Richardson, Virginia. John is in a good mood obviously. His letter is filled with good humor even when expounding and philosophizing.

I see by your card that you have begun to learn your trade. How do you like it? I hope that you will like it better than I do "soldiering." If you don't, you will never learn to "dress up." Sometimes we are told that we don't know enough to "right dress." I suppose we don't, but we know there is a good time coming. Thirteen months are not long, but that will number my days in blue Besides those two dresses we have three others. It will take a long time to wear them out, and I see they are made in the same fashion all over the civilized world...

You sometimes speak of folks getting married and going to be married and wedding days and all that sort of things. I suppose young women think of such things often. I don't know as I can blame them any, for I can't help thinking of such things once in awhile myself. But the more I think of it, the worse it will be for me, provided there is any goodness in a married life. I hear much said of single blessedness and I very naturally came to the conclusion that two good things are very seldom found in pairs. Therefore, if there should be any good, united to something wicked, why the result would be like uniting sweet and sour which would be spoiling the qualities of both. That would be making wicked worse and placing goodness on the same footing. There is no logic (can you see it). I am the person spoken of in "Mother Goose's Melodies" who never said a foolish thing and never said a wise one, so I hope you will pardon this awkward appoligy (sp) for a letter.

May 21, 1863 was the date of John's next letter. Nostalgia caused him to think back to better days.

I am glad to learn that you have to labor only eight hours each day for then you will have much time to yourself which will give you a chance of not only helping yourself and friends, but also to enjoy the pleasant summer evenings. I know the streets of New Haven must be splendidly shaded and a evening walk under those trees is something to be coveted...

The weather is splendid – quite warm for this time of year. We kept very busy doing all manner of work... We have to learn lessons in Artillery and recite twice a week which uses up much of my spare time. (We) drill twice a day and details on fatigue duty all the time.

I shall go on guard tomorrow morning. I am on guard once in five days. Two of our Companies were in those battles that took place near Fredricksburg.

A letter, dated June 14, 1863 arrived at Mary's door, starkly reaffirming that a war was being fought.

In the letter, John tells about an explosion at Ft. Lyon. The explosion noted occurred on June 9, 1863. A detail from the 3rd New York Artillery Battalion was managing ammunition and at the time was refilling shells with powder. The process required the existing powder, which had been exposed to moisture, to be removed with wooden spoons. The detail commander, concerned at the slow progress, issued metal priming wires to speed the removal. A spark from one of the priming wires rubbing against the cast iron shell case set off the explosion. Twenty-one men were killed in the blast and another ten injured...

There was an explosion in Ft. Lyon last Tuesday which killed *nearly thirty men, and wounded about fifteen more. It was garrisoned by the 3d N.Y. Artillery (German regt.) The fort is about six miles from here, but I could see it. All the powder in the magazine blew up.*

Department of Historic Resources

It made a cloud of dirt and smoke that could be seen for over twenty minutes. No one knows how it happened for the person who was so careless as to be the cause of it was blown up with it.

At the time of the accident, some companies of the 19th C.V. were practicing in the fort. We have target practice during this month with the Artillery.

And then, the good and disgruntled news...

I must not forget to tell you that I have been promoted. I am a Sergeant now. I think promotion goes quite slow in this company. In over a year, we have lost only one Sergt. He was discharged and the person who was promoted in his place got reduced soon after. It may be my fortune to be served up in the very same way, but I will try to do my duty. The only trouble we have is when on guard, the sergt. has charge of the guard and, if there should be prisoners and the least favor is shown them, off goes their sergt. stripes.

John's letter, dated July 14, 1863 was a commentary about recent events.

We are drilled as usual twice a day. Sometimes in the night we have to go and (lie) by our guns, but since Lee has fallen back to Williamsport, his raiders do not trouble us much. I guess Meade engages all his attentions at present and circumstance which does not make us jealous for our midnight sparking is something for which we are not over anxious.

The stricter draft laws that passed in March 1863 and the Conscription Act that allowed draft-eligible men to buy their way out of military service combined to cause dissent and rioting in New York City. In the month preceding the July 1863 draft lottery, antiwar newspaper editors published inflammatory attacks on the draft law aimed at inciting the white working class.

The rioters' targets initially included only military and governmental buildings, symbols of what was considered the unfairness of the draft. Mobs attacked only those individuals who interfered with their actions, but by the afternoon of the first day, some of the rioters had turned to attacks on black people, and on things symbolic of black political, economic and social power.

An 1863 illustration appearing in the *Illustrated London News*, depicting the fighting in the streets during the New York Draft Riots

John's commentary on events precipitated by the war and stricter laws, continued.

I need not congratulate you on the good fortune of the nation during the forepart of this month. I know that we are overjoyed at the news from our armies, but New York is acting a part which does not reflect much credit on its law-abiding citizens. I sincerely hope that the leaders in those riots will suffer death and that none of the guilty wretches will be shielded from justice. If such persons are not justly dealt with, we might as well give up the ship of State.

His next letter, written August 16, 1863, tells about the process and road to promotion.

Since I last wrote to you, I have been examined for a Lieut.cy and failed — that is quite encouraging, is it not! There is an inspector general who inspects these defenses. It is his duty to question the non-commissioned officers on artillery and send the names of the best-posted in each company to headquarters. My name was sent in once when I was a corporal and got to be a sergeant on account of it. We have had two such inspections and on the last one the officer told me that he would recommend me for promotion. I had to appear before a board of officers who met for the purpose of examining all who were recommended and have since learned that my name was among those who would have a commission, but it was placed in the last half of the list there being eight vacancies. But the Governor has reserved the right of appointing half himself so that my name was thrown off and that is all the good it has done me. If a person receives a commission, he cannot come home when the company and the regt. does but will have to stay until the war is over.

The weather is very hot and it seems as though we would melt some days. This makes the third summer of it and in all probability the last one which is quite consoling. We have just been paid off which will give us a chance to buy vegetables which will be quite a luxury for us.

The year of 1863 is waning. Fall is approaching. John's next letter is dated, September 27, 1863.

I am going to Washington (DC) tomorrow Providence permitting and I mean to see the Patent Office and the Smithsonian Institute. It will be a hard day's work and I think that I shall feel tired about this hour tomorrow night. It is quite a difficult job to get a pass to the City of Washington.

"Seven more months to serve," so the boys recon. It seems rather childish to talk that way but they will. We have good news from our armies — half of Meade's army has gone to reinforce Rosecrans. I think that in a few days Mr. Bragg & co. will have to go back and East Tennessee will be clear of rebel rule again. I think that Rosecrans' army will soon be over a hundred and fifty thousand.

In his October 25, 1863 letter, John discusses with Mary the ramifications of their close relatives being drafted.

I have just had a letter from father. He just heard that another of the royal race is in U.S. Army, viz. Thomas Layden. He (said) *he is in good health and is enjoying himself. I have just heard from Thomas — he tells me that he is not in good health and that he is going up country (in) a few days. He tells me Brannen is also in town — "Come out of the draft" Mr. B. or you may catch your death. I suppose he has the nightmare every night and sees great guns, cannon balls, gray backs, wooden legs and all that sort of things. I had rather die twice than to dread things both day and night. Don't tell him what I say for then there would be an earthquake in those regions. I have respect for both persons and property and would not like to bring about dire results.*

John has some important news to tell Mary in his November 21, 1863 letter, but he is feeling good and his words convey a light-hearted silliness.

What if you should see me in New Haven in the course of a few weeks? Tell Mr. Spring that I am going to re-enlist. By doing so I will get $700 and thirty days furlough. Now, I think thirty days furlough would be worth $700 besides, when I could have a chance to see all my friends. Perhaps they would not want to see me, but I could not help that. I want to see some of them...

You told me that Mr. Spring thanked me very much for my sympathy (for not being drafted) and said that he was exempt on account of a crucked toe. I think it is all owing to a rib. You have heard doubtless, or perhaps the minister read about Eve — how that she was made of a rib, etc. I well remember what a patriotic wife he has got, and I know how she (Spring's lady- not Eve) liked the Administration — and from that fact I think it must be owing to her that he is exempt — not to say that he has a crucked toe. He must be thinking of a rib for that you know is crucked... or perhaps instead of being formed like the rest of the world, she, through some unaccountable fault of nature, was made of a toe instead of a rib. I suppose as long as he has got her in tow he must be exempt. Poor fellow!

I am glad that I have no such toes, toe-heads, toe corns or any thing of the kind and so I know no reason why I should not go a soldiering another three years. So I am going to accept of $700 and a furlough and go home and come back. Out here we can get some of our faulty members amputated so that soldiering is not the worst trade out...

(I wasn't able to follow the rest of his light-hearted letter, but hopefully, you got the gist. If you want to read the full text, be sure to get a copy of John Dwyer's book with all of Captain John O'Brien's letters in it.)

December 9, 1863 was the last letter of the year that John wrote to Mary. In it, he tries to explain further some of his reasoning for re-enlisting after he had said, not too long before, that he would never re-enlist.

I barely hinted re-enlisting in my last (letter). I did not say that I had enlisted neither have enlisted yet, but before this letter reaches you I shall be enlisted for three years or during the war and, if Providence permits, I shall be in New Haven a week from tonight on a thirty day furlough. I shall not promise to be anywhere at any particular time. I am, nevertheless obliged to Susan (Mary's sister) for the invitation, but cannot accept it at present.

I suppose you will think my conduct strange and so it appears to me knowing well what a soldier's life is, and my time being so near to an end, a time to which I have looked hopefully for a long time, but still I have good prospects as long as I have health and life. I cannot hope to do better out of the army. I receive from the U.S. $402 and from the State $300 bounty and you know that I will have to work hard for a living if I was at home. It would take three years to boy up that doing the best that I could hope. Besides, I get now $20 per month and the present Congress is going to raise our pay at least .50 per cent. If I was a private I would not re-enlist; but still, I may, through improper conduct, become that. But, my chance is just as good for promotion if I behave myself. As long as I remain where I am I shall get along very well. I do no guard duty, no fatigue or picket duty and these are the hardest parts of a soldier's duties The reg't will be kept up, for a great many men have re-enlisted already and many more will. I may see the day that I shall be sorry for it but have never been sorry for going into the army and trust that I never will be. I only hope that God will give me health and strength to do my duty as a soldier.

I have an interest in the cause. I always advocated the great principles of freedom — the idea for which we are fighting. How would it look for me to leave the contest before it was finished? I could not do it. I should go into the army if I served out my present term of enlistment. If I was a married man it would be far different. I believe that, if such was my good fortune, I would stay at home. But, I never formed such an alliance; neither I have of any in prospect — a thing on which you were so good at guessing. In fact, I shall never get married until I get a salary of over a thousand dollars a year, and I suppose you may safely say that I shall never have such good luck. I never may if I loose life or limb in the service.

I am sorry to learn that Tom done as he has. I never expected anything of the kind. It has grieved me very much and as soon as I heard of (it) I immediately tried to get a furlough, but there was no hopes unless I do as I have done. I am anxious to see him and I shall try to get him into this regiment if I can if he remains in Conn. I think I can do it — at least I hope so. I cannot imagine what possessed him to enlist in any reg't but this. There is no arm of service as good as heavy artillery. Cavalry is better than infantry, but it is very hard for they are on the go all the time.

The "Tom" referred to in John's letter, above, is probably John's younger half-brother, Tom O'Brien, and it appears as though he was able to help him enlist with the 1st Connecticut Cavalry Regiment, if not the heavy artillery division — at least a Thomas O'Brien mustered into that regiment on November 25, 1863, according to military records.

I suppose my mother will not like to have me stay; neither will my father. I am sorry to disappoint them, but I long ago made up my mind.

John re-enlisted as a veteran on December 10, 1863, in Company F, 1st Connecticut Heavy Artillery, and on December 29, 1863, he was promoted to 2nd Lieutenant of Company A.

1st Connecticut Heavy Artillery Regiment; date and place unknown. (*Instructional Resources Corp. 2005*)

Drill at Fort Richardson. (*Library of Congress*)

Tent emcampment; Fort Richardson, Virginia. Date unknown. (*U.S. National Park Service*)

A federal picket line near Fort Stedman where John's company fought later in the war. (*Library of Congress*)

Chapter Five

The War Years - 1864

John's first letter of 1864, dated January 1, was rather short, but full of good news.

He spent Christmas Day, a Friday, with Thomas at Camp Cherbourgh. (***Note:*** I have not been able to determine if the Thomas of whom he speaks is his uncle, Thomas Layden, or his half-brother, Thomas O'Brien, nor can I find the location of a Camp Cherbourgh in Civil War sites, but it was probably a camp located near Washington, D.C.)

On Monday, December 28, 1863, he was commissioned as a 2nd Lieutenant of Company A of the 1st Connecticut Volunteer Heavy Artillery regiment. On Wednesday, he was able to visit family and friends in Washington, D.C. before reporting for duty at Fort Reynolds near Alexandria, Virginia.

(I was) *mustered in on Tuesday. I had a pass to Washington for 24 hours on Wednesday and have gone on duty today. I have not all my things here yet. We have a splendid mess where I am now. Our board only costs $10 per week* (and I) *have also splendid quarters. My outfit cost me $150.00.*

Non-commissioned officers from the 1st Connecticut Heavy Artillery regiment sitting down for a meal (mess). The second man on the right hand side with what looks like a boy leaning against him, looks a bit like John.

Settling in to his new situation must have taken some time, as John's next letter was dated March 28, 1864 and sent from Fort Reynolds.

I keep myself at work all the time. I have to study hard all my spare time (as) *I shall be examined soon again and am now preparing for it. When there are four more vacancies there will be a chance again for me and that will be about the 22nd of May. I am very anxious to pass a good examination. We have a delightful weather here at present. We have pickets out and we are watching for raids.*

John's letter of April 30, 1864 brings unwanted news as well as congratulations to Mary, who announced that she was to be married.[1]

---

[1] According to family history research, Mary Walker was married to James David Tennyson in a Protestant ceremony on March 31, 1864, but the "real" wedding in a Catholic church wasn't to take place until September 6, 1864.

I expect to go to the front in a few days. We are packing and getting ready for it. We do not know how soon that will be, but suppose it to be in the course of a couple of weeks. We are loading a siege train again – where we are going is a mere matter of speculation.

The weather is splendid and the leaves are beginning to show on the trees; apple trees have been in blossom some days.

When I last heard from Thomas, he was in West Virginia and had been in one skirmish. I have not heard from him during the last month, but suppose him to be at Harpers Ferry.

I have heard that the 6th is at Fortress Monroe and if our train goes down that way I may see Father.

Burnside's Corps (9th) has gone to the Army of the Potomac making that army about 35,000 stronger. Gilmore's Corps is said to be at Fortress Monroe, and if that is true, why then, I shall see it either on the Penninsular or on the south side of the James River.

We have been mustered for pay today. Every man must be seen on such a day. When I commenced this letter the prospect was good for fine weather now (3 o'clock p.m.) it is storming. Tomorrow brings around May 23rd of which the old men will go home. If I had not re-enlisted and had not been promoted, I would only have to stay twenty-three days, but I am not sorry.

Mary must wait for more news until John's next letter arrives on September 16, 1864, from Morton Battery near Petersburg, Virginia, but only because an earlier letter of John's never made it to her home.

I am surprised to learn that you did not receive an answer to your last letter. I have been looking for an answer to my last for two months. I asked Willie if he would inquire how it was that you had forgotten me. He has been silent on the subject and I had come to the conclusion that you were going to be married and was too busy to find time to remember your distant friend...

In the summer of '64 the 1st Connecticut Heavy Artillery regiment took to manning the works in the attempt to encircle the Rebel army at Petersburg, Virginia.

I tell you, this is a glorious place – a continual fourth of July – firing all the time.

Willie must have magnified my injuries for I told him I was only struck with a bullet from a spherical case on the morning of the 18th of August. It did not knock me from my feet even. It only made me step backwards a trifle. If it had come harder, it would have gave my friends evidence that I was facing the foe. An artillery man is very liable to be struck in the back. However, if I fall, I prefer to be struck where I was that morning — in the forehead.

We are very close to the enemy where we can hear them yell, see them load and point their guns, etc. I am within four hundred yards of the mined fort of Gen. Burnside. (I) was in the battle of the 30th of July the day it was blown up. I am very busy every day. (I) have any quantities of things to do and get but little thanks for it, but I must keep on (and) let it cost whatever it may until we are everywhere triumphant — the Union returned — and peace once more dwells in our land. The next time I see you, I mean, if it be God's will, to tell you many things which I have not now time to write of.

The next letter, also from Morton's Battery near Petersburg, Virginia arrives — this one dated October 14, 1864.

Now my dear friend, don't let my re-enlisting be the occasion of any trouble. I know this is not a safe place, but then there is nothing like being a man and doing one's duty so long as I live. I shall stay in the army always. I like the service. I expect to be promoted in the course of a month or, at the longest, two months hence, then I shall be mustered into the service for three years more, and cannot leave it if I wish, honorably. Some must do it. I may as well be here as others, and then others may have better reason for staying at home — a family for example. I tell you, although it may seem strange, I am content. I should like to see my friends often and if God is willing I shall go and see them this fall or winter. I am still entitled to twenty days and I shall have them, and hope for more. I am very sure that I could live happy out of the service, but then I am very well off and I have no reason to complain.

I am glad that Father has got back. He has had (a) very hard time of it. I might think different if I had to buffet around as infantry.

A corporal of our company was mortally wounded two days since. He died last night. His name was Jeremiah Sullivan. He was drilling recruits when he received his wound. He will be buried with military honors today.

On November 8, 1864, John was promoted to 1st Lieutenant, Company M of the 1st Connecticut Heavy Artillery regiment.

John's letter of November 16, 1864 from Battery No. 20, seemed to be more somber in tone. His concerns about family and friends at home revealed a deep loneliness—something very unusual for him to this point.

I have not heard from my father in a long time. I am glad to learn that he is well. Who told you that I thought of going home? If I did think of it, I have changed my mind since, if people will not write to me, I take it for granted they do not want to see me. So, I am going to stay at the front all the time, Providence permitting.

You may tell Susan that I would like to help her eat those mince pies you spoke of as being in preparation for Thanksgiving dinner, but I am very shy of company, so that I am glad that I am a soldier and far away.

If Abe had not been re-elected, I should feel very bad, but seeing that he has been re-elected for another term, I am happy even if my friends have forgotten me...

I am in a very lonely place now. Close to me is the celebrated Battery Sedgewick, more generally known as "Fort Hell!" I have a battery of big mortars here and every day we have to use them. Myself and a lieutenant, just promoted from a sergeant, have a bomb-proof and a wall tent for our place of abode. This lieutenant is a young Irishman. His name is Gardiner Reynolds and is from Meriden. He belongs to the Episcopal church also. He is a fine fellow, but then you don't want to know anything about him.

Apparently, Mary mentioned in one of her letters about getting cotton for her dressmaking business. It set off an unexpected reaction from John. Mary's great great grandson, John Dwyer, suspects that she must have bragged about being able to get some good Southern cotton and the only way she could have gotten it was if it had been smuggled through the blockade.

You are not at all welcome to that cotton. What you don't mean to say that you used that cotton and put it in somebody's ___word unreadable___. Well, well you are right. A dressmaker's skip is the right place, but then such things might bear a little investigation, but I don't prefer to get too much of that article in that way – *"a few pounds."* What do you mean? I have heard tell of the Battle of New Orleans and how Gen. Jackson used cotton bales for breast works. It is strange to think of how many different ways cotton may be used. At that time, it was our country's salvation, but it has been veryly the cause of the country's ruin. If there never was any cotton, there never would have been any war – no rebels – and here you are wishing for cotton and what would you do with it? I have heard of the secrets of a profession. Do you mean to turn traitor? or do I misunderstand? Please explain.

You can tell Kate that I was promoted on the 8th of November, the day that Abe beat "Little Mac." I belong to Company M." If you had not said so much about that cotton I would have had room to tell you lots of things but that has spoiled all.

Give my love to John Spring, Kate, M. Myers, Susan, and save part for yourself. I am very glad to hear that Quirk is a temperance man. It's (been a) *few days since I tried to find Tom Layden. I went to where his company was and he had been there that morning, but was at City Point at the time and is permanently detailed at the Hd-*(headquarters?) *of the reg't as saddler. His companions told me he is well. You know that he belongs to Co. D 15th N.Y. Vol Engineers.*

During the daytime we have no picket firing, but nights, it is very brisk. I am so close to the Johnnies that I can hear them talk when they speak to our pickets. I can hear caps explode when their guns do not go off. They are only about as far from my mortars as from Rose Court to Lafayette St. – *about two hundred yards is the propper* (sp) *distance.*

John seems to be in much better spirits with his next letter dated December 27, 1864 – most probably because he was no longer on the battle front. His letter bears the return address of Battery 4 near Petersburg, Virginia via Fortress Monroe.

I received your kind letter in due time, but I have been on the move since I received and could not find time to answer. I have left where shell and bullets were flying so thick all the time, and I am now in command of a company of one hundred and thirty-eight men and two commissioned officers, I shall remain in command all the winter

I am very sorry I am not home. I have had an invitation from a nice young lady to go a-skating. I would like to go, but I cannot.

On December 19, 1864, he was transferred to Company I of the 1st Connecticut Heavy Artillery regiment.

I have been changed from Co. A to M and of late I have been changed from M to I and have all the batteries which this Co. I mans under my charge. The celebrated thirteen-inch mortar, the "Dictator," and the heavy guns known as the "Petersburg Express," are now commanded by your humble servant. The Dictator," however, is not in position, but is at City Point, but if it should be used, I would have it. I have been expressing packages to the cars which runs from Richmond to Petersburg today. One burst near a house. I know it must have had a woman in it. I was very sorry – the shot went over the train too much. I think you would not like to be disturbed that way?

You ask..."I suppose you wonder what I was going to do with so much cotton?" I heard Susan say she was going to make some bed quilts"xxx

Cheer up. Sherman captured 25,000 bales in Savannah. I am so glad, for the young ladies will not pine away now. Shaw! you can't turn that off that way. I never laughed so much in my life as I did when I read that...

Three officers of the 1st Connecticut Heavy Artillery regiment. The officer standing in front of the tree is believed to be Capt. John O'Brien. There is no way to tell for sure. (*Library of Congress*)

Descendant, John Dwyer, had the two photos above run through a face-recognition software program and the similarities that it found between them are shown here.

A mortar gun set up in the Siege of Petersburg, Virgiinia. (*Wikimedia*)

Parrot guns outside nearby Fort Brady

Entrance to a bombproof magazine storage bunker at Fort Brady, Virginia, an earthworks fort located near Fort Richardson. (*Library of Congress*)

Battery (Ft.) Sedgewick, aka "Fort Hell." (*Library of Congress*)

Chapter Six

The War Years - 1865

On January 26, 1865, John O'Brien put in for a 30-day leave of absence for the purpose of visiting friends in Connecticut.

I was mustered into the United States service on the 8th of November for three years. I have been in the service since the 22nd of May 1861, and I have been absent eleven days since the last named date. I am Very respectfully your obt. servant, John O'Brien, 1st. Lt. 1st. Conn. Arty.

The next letter that Mary received, then, was dated March 7, 1865 and was just a short, friendly letter expressing his thanks and to let her know that he had returned to Battery 4 "before Petersburg, Virginia" safely.

According to John Dwyer, the O'Brien family's historian, "In March 1865, the Confederate General John Gordon proposed to Lee that he attempt a breakout assault on the Union entrenchments. O'Brien's command at Battery No. 4 was just to the north of the point of attack and was well placed to do damage."

On March 25, 1865, John's company took part in the Battle of Fort Stedman, also known as the Battle of Hare's Hill.

The Union Army fortification in the siege lines around Petersburg, Virginia, was attacked in a pre-dawn Confederate assault by troops led by Maj. Gen. John B. Gordon. *The attack was the last serious attempt by Confederate troops to break the Siege of Petersburg. After an initial success, Gordon's men were driven back by Union troops... commanded by Maj. Gen. John G. Parke.* (Wikipedia)

On March 26, 1865, John filed an official report as the commander of Battery 4 to Lieut. W. S. Maloney, A.A.A.-G. Siege Batteries, "before Petersburg, Virginia."

I have the honor to submit the following report of the part sustained by Co. "I" 1st Conn. Art'y, the garrison of Battery No. 4, during the engagement of yesterday.

At four o'clock in the morning, I heard firing on the line near Battery No. 4, but supposed it to be wholly confined to the pickets. At half past five, an hour and a half later, I saw indications that an advance had been made by the enemy upon our lines near Battery No. 10. I had the company under arms and made arrangements for a defense, when I received orders to open on the enemy, who were now in possession of Fort Stedman and Battery No. 10. These orders where received at daylight. I fired one-hundred and thirty [130] rounds of percussion and six [6] rounds of time fuze shell, nearly all of which were thrown into an advancing column of the enemy which was in the rear of the last named work. About fifteen shell were thrown into the Chesterfield Battery. This battery opened upon Battery No. 6 and the line of works near it. Six shell were thrown into a retreating column of the enemy when it was on the plain in front of Battery No. 9. Fearing an advance in case of the failure of a pending charge of our forces, fired only when the enemy troops were in sight, having only about one hundred rounds for each piece [three pieces].

On the same day, he wrote to Mary.

You will learn before this reaches you that we had a fight here yesterday. The enemy took our lines near Fort Steadman directly in front of my battery and they advanced rapidly to within five hundred yards of me when they were stopped by a line of battle. They had possession of our works from five o'clock in the morning until about nine when our troops advanced in glorious style, recapturing all our lost ground and artillery. I had a good opportunity to give the "Johnnies" cold iron and the only reason why I did not scatter more is that my ammunition was not enough for a long action. The enemy lost in prisoners, twenty-five hundred men. Our killed, wounded and missing is four hundred and eighty nine. Our dead was not so much as the enemy whose losses must have been about two thousand. We did not have that number of men in the lines. I am writing before eight in the morning. The battery was under arms at 3:30, fearing another attack.

Shortly afterwards, on April 9, 1865, he was declared a Captain by Brevet and assigned as commander of Company I.

Interestingly, during the American Civil War, almost all senior officers received some form of brevet award, mainly during the final months of the war. These awards were made for gallantry or meritorious service, rather than for command.

Despite his being in battle, John made sure that he kept up his correspondence. His next letter to Mary, dated April 3, 1865, was very short without many pleasantries.

We have been fighting very hard and now we have the City (Richmond). I was in the fight of the 25th and have had men killed and wounded. My men turned the enemy's guns upon them in their own forts yesterday.

Three days later, on April 6, 1865, John found more time to write, for he was back in his old training grounds at Fort Richardson, Virginia.

I have just received your letter and I am very glad to hear from you and all my friends. Tell John Spring to go to Cummins and sware at him for me. He made my pistol case so poor that the buttin (sp) broke and while riding to support Gen. Wilcox Saturday night, I lost it. I was in such a hurry that I could not stop to look for it, for I had just received a programme of Sunday's battle and I had men, guns and ammunition to move to cover the charge about to be made.

Well, what does Kate say now about Uncle Abe? He was down here. We have Richmond as well as Petersburg. I shall tell you all about our fighting some day, Providence permitting.

John's letter continues in a light-hearted banter since the heavy fighting has dwindled and the prospects for the end of the war are on everyone's minds. He even speaks of the young women in the area.

Tell Mr. Myers and Spring that it is a good time to enlist – the war will soon be over. I suppose Kate and Susan will not object. Ah! no, I guess not. I am going to Richmond in a few days.

Since I commenced writing I have had an invitation to call and see a gentleman and lady by the name of Loram... They are Irish. Loram owns three large houses and any quantities of tobacco. He invested all his money in that and he is now doing his best to keep it. Mr. Malony has been there several times and I expect a good time when I go, for they are going to invite a young lady friend.

The girls here are good looking. They wear the best kind of clothes and when we ask them how they can do it, they say that they wore out all their old clothes and have nothing else to wear. The army is about thirty miles from here.

May 6, 1865 brings more hopes of being home soon. This time, John writes from Camp Near Port, Walthall Junction, Virginia, with tongue-in-cheek.

Well I suppose you imagine I'm happy to think I am going home... Tell her (Kate) that I have about made up my mind to elope with a damsel of the Sesech persuasion. By the way, there are lots of them here – nice ones too. Tell Cousin Kate I think I will bring home one, to see how she likes her. Tell Spring and Myers that I am so sorry they are married for I could introduce them to large plantations here. I suppose Johnson is bargained for? Poor fellow how I pity him. I am coming home in a month – some time in June.

By June, however, John's plans have changed, once again. In his letter dated June 7, 1865, from Depot Semmes, Virginia, he mentions his plans.

Your letter came in on time. You thought that I would not write any more letters to you before I came home, but I expect that I shall not come home this year, so that I may as well keep up the correspondence unless you see fit to drop it.

I have lots of fun here – plenty of nice young ladies and lots of time to talk to them. The weather is awful, and to keep cool requires much patience.

How would you like it if you should never see your humble servant again – that is to live in New Haven. I don't believe I will stay there long.

John was discharged as a Captain by Brevet for the U.S. Army on September 25, 1865.

That was the last letter in Mary's collection that she received from John.

To sum up John's military service, I will once again quote from the *Pacific Union Printer* article published in 1892 by the San Francisco Typographical Union No. 21.

He (Captain John O'Brien) w*as in the fortifications before Washington with his regiment, in the critical times when the nation's capital was threatened, and it was upon him, and such as he, that the nation counted for its safety. Very nearly all of the time of his service in the army, however, was spent in Virginia, between Washington and Petersburg and Richmond, with the Army of the Potomac, excepting six months in Maryland and three weeks in Pennsylvania, when Lee made his great raid to threaten the northern cities. He was in all the battles of the Peninsular Campaign, excepting the battle of Fair Oaks, and in all those, including the siege of Richmond and Petersburg, fought west of and including that of Fort Sedgewick, known to the Soldiers as Fort Hell, to the left of the celebrated Jerusalem road. The war closed with the fall of Richmond, and John O'Brien, who had enlisted as a private, was mustered out a first lieutenant and brevet captain, with the reputation of having performed splendid service in command of a battery at the siege of Richmond.*

Chapter Seven

After the War - Montana

It is believed that after the war, John O'Brien returned to New Haven for a short while before spreading his wings to explore opportunities offered in the West. He revealed some of his longings to travel in that letter he wrote to Mary on June 21, 1862.

I almost wish I was a free man again so that I could travel, for there is nothing under the sun that would please me better and as soon as this War is over I shall go and see the world somewhere.

We know little of his first adventures as he made his way westward, but the *Pacific Union Printer* newsletter of 1892 gives us some insight.

He (Captain John O'Brien) *went back to New Haven and his interrupted trade, still a young man, after the war; but the excitement of campaigning had bred in him that restlessness that has become the leading characteristic of Americans – he had earned the right to that nationality now – and, in April, 1866, he drew his card from the New Haven Union, and started for the golden Mecca in the west of all restless men, crossing the northern plains via the Bozeman cut off.*

Even in that far western land, where many men found it convenient to forget the virtues of a more civilized life, he was true to his principles as a friend of organized labor, quickly becoming one of the leaders in Helena Typographical Union, and serving as its corresponding secretary during the winter of 1866-67, during which time he worked on the Herald of Helena. *For two years following that winter he followed the business of freighting and mining, but the* (printing) *craft had laid its fascination upon* (him) *in his boyhood days, and he could not shake off the charm now.*

When John O'Brien arrived in Montana in 1866, he probably did so as a freighter of goods to supply the bustling mining town of Helena with needed commodities. Gold had been discovered there two years before. The boom-town, likened to the Nevada gold-rush town of Virginia City, was first called Last Chance Gulch, but on October 30, 1864, it was renamed "Helena." It's even possible that John even tried a bit of gold mining himself, before he returned to printing, the trade he learned as a young man.

Mule-drawn freight wagon in Helena, Montana 1870. (postcard)

On a website called "Helena As She Was," it tells of the most-likely route that John took when freighting goods into the Helena area:

During Helena's early years, (a) toll road, originating at the head of Missouri River navigation at Fort Benton, was the main shipping route into the area. Heavy rain and snow sometimes made the canyon road impassable.

In 1865, the Territorial Legislature granted a license to the Little Prickly Pear Wagon Road Company to build a toll road through the canyon. A year later, in 1866, Helena merchants James King and Warren Gillette bought the road and spent $40,000 upgrading it. By then traffic on it between Fort Benton and Helena had become so heavy, that the men were able to recoup their expenditure within two years.

By the early 1870s, it was part of the Benton Road, an important freight and passenger route in the territory. Thereafter, other roads and a railroad were constructed through the Prickly Pear Canyon.

During the winter of 1864 and the year 1865, hundreds of homes were built and the town grew to over 3,000 residents. A history, written by M. Murray Schreiner was published in the *Montana Magazine of History*, and included a description of the town, just a year before John arrived.

Much of the lumber used in Helena in the winter and spring of 1865 was hand sawed and eager men waited to seize every board as fast as sawed, at any price the owner might see fit to charge. The usual price generally agreed upon was twenty five cents per foot in gold dust.

...Before that time, flour had been arriving in small quantities and in May as little as ten pounds, which retailed at $1.10 per pound, was parceled out to the needy customers. Food stuff was scarce. One man paid $7.00 for a loaf of bread, and potatoes sold on the street at sixty cents a pound. A small quantity of seed wheat was eagerly purchased at forty cents per pound, to be used instead of rice. The people were crying that if the merchants would only bring in the goods, they would pay the price.

The town was filled with large, newly excavated holes that miners, searching for gold, dug within feet of homes. These holes were sometimes vast and even undermined some of the structures, themselves.

One account included in the *Montana Magazine of History* piece included the story of a Mrs. A. Combs who went outside her house one afternoon and fell into a fifty-foot deep prospector's hole *which had been sunk within ten feet of her cabin door. The woman sustained a broken thigh and was otherwise bruised. Dr. Turner and Dr. Mason were called immediately and Mrs. Combs was soon pronounced to be out of danger. That was the third or fourth such accident caused by the reprehensible habit of leaving deep prospect holes and shafts, unsurrounded by any barrier, in the midst of the most thickly populated portion of the town. The people were enraged and demanded that something be done about it, but they were slow to get action.*

By the time that John arrived in 1866, the town had built bridges over excavations along the mined-out Main Street so that travelers could pass along it.

These, then were the conditions that brought Captain John O'Brien to Montana and how he lived for the next year while working — probably as a typesetter or printer — with the area newspaper, the *Helena Herald*, and as one of the early officers of the Helena Typographical Union.

Unfortunately, the early beginnings of the Helena Typographical Union have been lost, but a newspaper article in the *Tri-Weekly Republican* stated that the Helena Typographical Union was organized on August 5, 1866. Permanent officers were elected: President, S.P. Bassett; Vice-President, J.L. Laird; Corresponding and Recording Secretary, I.H. Morrison; and Financial Secretary and Treasurer, D.S. Stanley.

Since John referred to his work as corresponding secretary with the union in the *Pacific Union Printer* piece, it is assumed that he had a major role in the issuance, almost six months later on February 19, 1867, of the first charter in Montana to a typographical union based in Helena. The charter was issued by the National Typographical Union to Helena Printers Union No. 95. This charter gave jurisdiction over the printing craft throughout the Montana territory.

While earning his wages as a printer for the local *Helena Herald* and possibly the earlier *Montana Radiator* of Helena, which ceased operation in late 1866, he most likely was also working to ensure that the printers throughout the territory were fairly represented.

It appears, however, that his two jobs must have clashed badly and may have precipitated his leaving Montana.

On October 19, 1867, just a month after John left for California, *The Montana Post*, a bitter rival of the *Helena Herald*, published a newspaper article headlined, "Printers Beware!"

Apparently, the pay scale of $1.00 per thousand ems[1], set by the union for printers, was not honored by the *Helena Herald* and as a consequence, the printers walked off their jobs. In retribution, the newspaper began *trying to supply their place with 'rats,' or unfair workmen,* according to the article.

The union issued a statement to the *The Montana Post*.

This is to warn all printers and the public, that we, the Helena Typographical Union, denounce the Herald *as a "rat office." On last Saturday night, the union made a reduction of fifteen cents per thousand ems on composition voluntarily, without even being approached by the proprietors on the subject, placing the rates at one dollar. The Herald now refuses to pay over seventy-five cents per thousand ems, and a "strike" is the consequence. We call upon all mechanics, and every one interested and in favor Union movements, to withdraw their patronage from a concern that, with the Whitlatch Union Mine to back it, refuses reasonable compensation to its workers. By order of the Helena Typographical Union No. 95... S.P. Basset, Pres't.*

John missed out on his first union strike, but it obviously solidified his belief in unions and their benefits to the working men and women. It was just the beginning of a lifetime devoted to helping oversee the formation of trade unions all over the country.

---

[1] "em:" the width of a piece of type about as wide as it is tall used as a unit of measure of typeset matter

Birdseye view of Helena, Montana, looking north; 1867.
(*Montana Historical Society Legacy Photograph Collection*)

Last Chance Gulch in 1865 when Capt. John O'Brien arrived.
(*Montana Travel*)

Last Chance Gulch. (*Legends of America*)

Corner of Main Street and Broadway, looking south. ~1865-1868
(*Montana Historical Society Legacy Photograph Collection*)

Mule-drawn covered freight wagons on Vawter Street, Helena, Montana. ~1874. (*Montana Historical Society Legacy Photograph Collection*)

Main Street, Helena, Montana. 1868
(*Montana Historical Society Legacy Photograph Collection*)

Chapter Eight

Next Stop: California

In September 1867, with his life's course set, John made his way to Sacramento, California. The *Pacific Union Printer* article continues.

He returned to the case, and presently he arrived in Sacramento, depositing a card there of the Helena Union. From this move dates his identification with union affairs in California and the Pacific Coast.

While in Sacramento, John O'Brien realized his dream of becoming a naturalized citizen of the United States. A California state voter's registration biographical card shows that he was naturalized on September 18, 1868 and became a registered voter the next day, on September 19, 1868.

From his letters, one can tell that John loved his country and had become a true patriot. He fought for the United States of America and he was willing to give his life in defending the principles he believed in. This was the final step in making it official.

John was only in Sacramento for a year when he left for San Francisco where he met his future bride. On June 15, 1869, he and Julia Agnes Healey (sometimes spelled "Haley") were married by Father Pindegrast in the St. Mary's Catholic Cathedral. St. Mary's later burned down during the Great San Francisco Earthquake of 1906. Their marriage record was destroyed, but fortunately, Julia included information about herself on her Widow's Pension Declaration application on which she listed all three priests as having married them.

Little other information is known of Julia's earlier life, although we know from the application that she was born in Ireland on April 3, 1849. I found a 1860 census record from Springfield, Hampden County, Massachusetts that looks like it might be her family. It lists her parents as Patrick (a laborer, age 45) and Catherine Healey (age 41) and their children Morris (18), Patrick (16), Margaret (13), Julia (11), Ella (8), Catharine (7), Johanna (5) and Thomas (3). Another son, John, was born to them in 1861. The family emigrated to the United States from Kilkenny, Ireland, arriving in Boston on June 12, 1849 when Julia was but 2 months old.

The Pacific Union Printer biography continues:

From Sacramento he (John) *came to San Francisco, bringing a card from the Sacramento Union. This was in 1869, and so commanding was the position he at once assumed that, at the time of the great strike of 1870, less than one year after his arrival here* (San Francisco), *Captain O'Brien held the trusted position of financial secretary of Eureka Union.*

The "great strike of 1870" to which the *Pacific Union Printer* refers is probably the North Adams Labor Strike of 1870 which actually began in Massachusetts, but involved San Francisco, and spread to other parts of the country, as well.

A group of employees at the Calvin T. Sampson's shoe factory in North Adams, Massachusetts went on strike in April 1870. They not only wanted higher wages, but they felt that they should only have to work a 10-hour workday instead of the normal (at that time) 12-hour day. The owner fired all of them and brought in replacements from a nearby town. Pressure was put on the replacements by the union and they quit. Sampson then sent his factory superintendent to San Francisco, California with orders to bring back 75 Chinese laborers. This precipitated union strikes all across the country and the use of Chinese labor remained a topic of contention between labor and management for quite some time.

While John became more and more involved in workers' rights in his trade, he and Julia soon started a family. Their first child, a son, William O'Brien, was born on April 18, 1870, followed by a daughter, Catherine "Katie" O'Brien, born on August 31, 1871[1]. Elizabeth L. "Lizzy" arrived on June 1, 1873.

In 1873 or 1874, according to the pension application that John filled out in 1915, he obtained 160 acres near the headwaters of the Siuslaw River in Lane County, Oregon, under the Homestead Act of 1862—which John called "the Soldier's Act" in his application.

The Homestead Act of 1862 served in part as a recruiting inducement for the Union Army. After the Civil War, a soldier was allowed to deduct the number of years that he served in the Union Army from the five-year homestead residency requirement.

---

[1] This is another discrepancy of dates connected with the O'Brien family. Katie's date of birth is listed as August 31, 1868 on her obituary, but census records support the 1871 year of birth.

Even after John obtained the land in Oregon, the O'Briens continued to live in San Francisco where he was running the Typographical Union. I cannot document it, but I believe that John took occasional hiatuses and visited his property in Oregon to build a home and clear it for farming, hoping to take his family there eventually.

A set of twins, Julia and Margaret, were born on October 5, 1874, but tragically, they died of diphtheria in June 1876 before they had attained their 2nd birthday.

The *Pacific Union Printer* article continues...

During all the troublous days of the great strike, Captain O'Brien stood in the forepart of battle, and in 1876 he was one of the brave men who organized the Federated Trades Assembly here, and so put the laboring man in a position to respect himself and to command respect as a man whose rights it was dangerous to infringe upon.

Federated Trades Assemblies were formed locally to represent many different trades unions. Each sent delegates to the meetings in order to give each a stronger stance and a more united front and local branches were established all over the U.S. They grew out of the movement that resulted in establishment of the Federation of Organized Trades and Labor Unions.

In the years 1873 to 1878, the U.S. was in a major depression. Trades unions held a national convention on November 15, 1881, and formed the Federation of Organized Trades and Labor Unions. The convention was held in Pittsburgh, Pennsylvania and was attended by "107 delegates from eight national unions, 11 city labor federations, 42 local craft unions, and three district and 46 local assemblies of the Knights of Labor. The International Typographical Union had the largest trade union delegation, with 14 attendees." It is assumed that John was among them.

The result was that labor unions were strengthened, but with the influx of Marxists and Socialists who tried to dictate union laws, they were becoming very political. Influential newspapers began to lobby to suppress the political power of the trade unions. Others, who wanted the unions to remain strong, but without the political connotations, began to implement a new form of Unionism which would free unions from political affiliation and limit their goals to the day-to-day concerns of working people.

Samuel Gompers was one of the foremost leaders of this New Unionism program. He and those backing him proposed that the organization restrict its membership to skilled craft unions, excluding those that supported unskilled workers. His resolution was adopted and the Federation of Organized Trades and Labor Unions was joined by Canada, as well.

The Committee on Organization which Samuel Gompers served on also proposed several other popular resolutions which also passed. These included: 1) legal incorporation of unions; 2) mandatory education of children; 3) prohibition of child labor under the age of 14; 4) apprenticeship laws; 5) the establishment of an 8-hour workday; 6) repeal of state conspiracy laws which did not provide a safe harbor for labor unions; 7) establishment of a federal agency to collect labor statistics; 8) abolition of convict labor; 9) prohibition of the importation of foreign workers; 10) federal legislation requiring ventilation and inspection of mines; 11) support for Irish liberation; 12) legislation making employers responsible for industrial accidents; and 13) a high protective tariff.

The New Unionism philosophy led by Samuel Gompers was established and named the American Federation of Labor (AFL) and it became a continuation of the Federation of Organized Trades and Labor Unions without the Marxist and Socialist political clout.

Local branches were formed in major cities and called themselves Federated Trades Assemblies. John O'Brien worked with the Federated Trades Assembly of San Francisco mentioned in the *Pacific Union Printer* article above.

Chapter Nine

On to Oregon

In 1879, the family left San Francisco, California and moved to the Oregon homestead near the Siuslaw River where they lived for a few years. [1] Another daughter, Joanna or "Anna," was born on August 20, 1879 after they arrived.

The homesteaded land became John's retreat in later years. Whenever he felt the need to escape the rigors and stress that built through his work, he always came back to his farm in Lorane to relax and regenerate.

In November 1880, the O'Brien's last child Ellen "Nellie" was born.

According to the information that John supplied on his Pension application, the family moved to Portland in December 1886 when he joined the staff of the *Oregonian* newspaper as a typesetter.

He had not lost interest in the plight of the working man, however, and he transferred his union card from San Francisco to the International Typographical Union No. 58 of Multnomah

---

[1] In 1887, the growing community became the town of Lorane. The area where the land lay is on what is now along Letz Creek Road.

County, Oregon. The following year, in 1888, he was named to the executive committee of the trade union where he served before being elected president of the union in 1889. He held that position until August 1892 when he retired from the presidency at his own request. He then rejoined the executive committee and served on it from 1893-1894.

In the book, *Union Democracy: The Internal Politics of the International Typographical Union* (1957), the International Trade Union of which #58 was a part, *had a unique system of factional opposition in its democratic elections. The local scale committees worked for a decent wage while the executive council sent ITU representatives to assist local unions in contract negotiations. All contracts had to be approved and ratified by both the Executive Council and the newspaper publisher. For most of its history, the ITU benefitted from friendly and strong competition between Independents and Progressives for control of the union.*

The *Pacific Union Printer* article of 1892, goes on to describe John's involvement in trade unions.

In January 1888, Multnomah Union sent Mr. O'Brien as a delegate to the Federated Trades Assembly of Portland, and it was natural that he should be selected by that body for high office. He served one term as vice-president of the Assembly, and was then elevated to the Presidency, which position he has held now for three years, and is likely to hold for as long as his strength or his inclination lasts.

During his tenure as president of the Multnomah Typographical Union No. 58 and with the Federated Trades Assembly of Portland, there is little doubt that he played a major role in the passage of the bill establishing Labor Day as a national holiday. Oregon was the first state in the nation to pass its own bill on February 21, 1887.

An interesting note is that when the city's Federated Trades Assembly was formed, it was AFL President Sam Gompers who came to Oregon in the 1880s to personally oversee its establishment and Gompers developed a great respect for John's work.

He specifically mentioned John O'Brien in his book *Seventy Years of Labor*.

> *In Portland, I met Captain John O'Brien, a very able man, one of the chief editors on the Portland* Oregonian *in addition to being a staunch trade union man.*

It's interesting to note that Gompers referred to John as "one of the chief editors" of the *Oregonian*. That was never established in all of the research that I did. He was a printer by trade.

Through the years, Gompers wrote a series of papers reflecting his vision for unions that would provide the best support and protection of the American worker. In a 1974 compilation of his papers, John O'Brien's biosketch was included, and he was listed as one of the AFL's leading activists in the labor movement.

A newspaper article printed in the *Portland Morning Oregonian*, dated April 24, 1888, tells of his work with the union.

> *The plan for Labor Day celebration has been changed to a mass meeting of labor in the evening. Capt. John O'Brien, Shaw and Montag were appointed to a committee on Music and Hall to ascertain the cost and report at the next meeting.*

During this time, John was commuting back and forth between the family home in Portland and the Lorane homestead. I'm not sure how much work he was able to do in Lorane, for his life in Portland was rather busy.

On April 25, the day after the *Morning Oregonian* article came out, the Democratic primary election to select delegates to the Multnomah County convention chose John O'Brien as its delegate from Precinct 3 in the North Portland District. It turned out to be a very lively event before the evening was through, as reported by the *Morning Oregonian.*

> *There seemed to be an organized opposition to what the kickers called "Eugene Protzman's damned reform ticket," the most demonstrative fellow being a big, dirty loafer named Tom Moore, a hanger-on around some brothel. He was strongly opposed to reform of any kind and had a small following who cried, "Down with the ring ticket; we've got no use for these people; we are going to get even on them," etc. Finally, Joseph Hughes was about to thrash this loafer when both of them were arrested by Policeman Holsapple, and quiet was restored for the time.*

Presently, A. Noltner stepped up to vote, and Riley, the fellow who stood up to be knocked down by David Campbell, seized him and tried to pull him away from the poll. A. Noltner, Jr., who was one of the judges, leaped over the table and struck Riley, knocking him down. Then Riley's father grabbed Noltner, Sr., who whacked him over the head with a cane in a very energetic manner, when the bystanders separated the combatants.

To say the least, John's entrance into politics had a rather unusual beginning. It seems that the proceedings continued to take on interesting twists.

On April 28, 1888, at the Multnomah Democratic Convention, a *Sunday Oregonian* newspaper article described the following day under the headline, "The Multnomah Democrats Hold a Glorious Convention." John was named to a seat on the Central Committee to represent Precinct 3 in the North Portland District.

During the convention, a motion was made that further proceedings be adjourned and postponed for a week out of respect for the recent death of Portland Mayor John Gates.

According to the article, *Before the motion was put, Finnerty moved that a committee of three be appointed to draft fitting resolutions on the death of Mayor John Gates.*

The motion carried and a committee of three was appointed. Another motion was made that before the adjournment, precinct officers should be selected.

A round of applause followed when John O'Brien moved that the convention proceed with the regular order of business. The motion was seconded and the suggested adjournment was questioned.

Murphey, the member who seconded John's motion, asked why the adjournment was proposed. He felt that *the most important business was the appointment of a central committee and it was necessary for the candidates to know who would manage the campaign.*

O'Brien said the convention had done good work thus far and *ought to finish the work at once. He regarded the movement to adjourn as unusual, not to say, questionable.*

*There was some wrangle about parliamentary rules and finally, as a way out, a motion to adjourn until Tuesday was made and lost, 28 to 20. A motion to adjourn for **five minutes** prevailed, 28 to 15.*

The convention article was quite long and I won't try to quote more, but it is an example of the outspoken and respected role Capt. O'Brien assumed in the proceedings.

John spent a great deal of time during this period, conducting and attending International Typographical meetings, both local and national, and Federated Trades Assembly meetings which were local branches of the Federation of Organized Trades and Labor Unions. He was asked to speak at quite a few.

A July 10, 1888 article appearing in the *Morning Oregonian*, tells of John being elected President of the Federated Trades Assembly, and his speech addressing his thanks and visions for it. The article could perhaps hold some kind of record for publishing the longest single sentence written by a journalist in a major newspaper of the day.

Capt. O'Brien, on taking the chair, thanked the delegates for the honor they had conferred upon him in placing him in the chair. He gave credit to the retiring president and officers for the able manner in which they had filled their several stations, called attention to the progress that has been made in trades union organization and the good accomplished during their term of office, and that it would be the aim of the assembly to so conduct its business as to keep secure all that they have done, and that he had hoped a good relationship would be maintained with the employers and that and in their deliberations with them the sober second thought would prevail.

On August 5, 1888, an article appeared in the *Morning Oregonian*, giving an insight into John's philosophy. It was a meeting of the Baker's Union, and Captain John O'Brien and two other men, who represented the Federated Trades Assembly, were asked to address the group.

Captain O'Brien spoke on the advantages of trade unions which, he said, protected men from the greedy and selfish employer who aims solely to reduce wages.

Other newspaper articles tell of John serving on committees as an ambassador of the International Typographical Union

#58 of Portland, greeting important visitors invited to speak at the meetings.

In September 1888, the Portland union was ranked 33rd "in point of membership" out of 200 unions in the United States, Canada and the Sandwich Islands. (*the Sandwich Islands... aka Hawaii?*)

During this time, while he was making such an impact on trade union business, he was also working as a "compositor," or typesetter, for Portland's largest newspaper, the *Oregonian*. Some resources describe him as a reporter for the paper for many years, but I believe them to be incorrect.

The Federated Trades Assembly in Multnomah County, was strong and very active during John's tenure. A December 21, 1888 article in the *Morning Oregonian*, quoted John's opening address at a mass meeting which not only included the Federated Trades Assembly, but the Knights of Labor groups, as well.

The chairman (Captain John O'Brien) *stated that the assembly proposed to give open meetings with a view of discussing political questions that could not be considered in the different unions, for the purpose of securing national and state legislation in the interests of workingmen; to secure public opinion in favor of organized labor; to secure the formations of local unions; for considering measures for lessening the friction between capital and labor; and promoting friendly feelings between employees and employers.*

The *Eugene City Guard* carried a complimentary article copied from the January 1, 1889 edition of the *Union Printer* of San Francisco — probably the *Pacific Union Printer* — on January 12, 1889. Titled "Both Well Known Here," it talks about both John O'Brien, President, and W.F. Osburn, Secretary and Treasurer of the Federated Trades Assembly No. 58. Each had just been re-elected to office.

The Federated Trades Assembly of Portland is presided over by Capt. John O'Brien, a member of No. 58. He is also Chairman of our Executive and Arbitration Committee, where most of the work of the union is accomplished, and serves the American Federation of Labor as Organizer for the Northwest. The time, attention and effort demanded by the numerous duties that Mr. O'Brien must perform are no small sacrifice in behalf of the cause of labor, and he has the confidence, not only of his own Union, but all represented in the Federation. The weekly papers that were induced to come into the Union in the past year were taken hold of by the Federated Trades with success. In general, there is more thorough and extensive organization of labor in Oregon than heretofore, and the prospect is cheerful...

On February 16, 1889, the *Morning Oregonian* published a letter to the editor entitled "The Ungrateful Brother; The Bull Run Water Bill from a Labor Standpoint," written by Capt. John O'Brien. At the end of his letter, he included a letter sent to him by M.H. O'Connor of Salem, Oregon, followed by John's rebuttal.

I have decided to share the exchange in this book as it gives a detailed insight into not only the situation, but the man, himself, and his beliefs regarding his union work. **Please note,** however... the newspaper scan was extremely poor with whole words missing from some of the text. I believe that I have transcribed most of it correctly, but there are places indicated with question marks that are purely guesses on my part. Other parts with an underline are places where I didn't even feel comfortable hazarding a guess, so I will leave those portions to our readers' imaginations...

February 11, 1889. Monday, February 11, the day set apart at Salem to endeavor to pass the Bull Run water bill over the governor's veto had the appearance in this city of a day when important election returns were coming in – so intense was the interest in the measure before the house. The bill was one with which I was in full sympathy, believing that if it passed over the governor's veto, every dollar of the $1,500,000 would be honestly spent among the business men, mechanics, and laborers of this city. I was not in sympathy with those who objected to the bill in the form it came up for final passage. As regards taxation of the bonds, I don't hold that to be a labor question. The form that would insure the investment of home capital is unquestionably the best, and knowing how much it would add to the very many advantages which our city already possesses to have plenty of pure water. Also, in response to courteous appeals from *my colleagues and my own personal feeling, I forwarded a dispatch which was read by Hon. W.B. Gilbert, in his admirable address delivered on that day in support of the bill and for that address, I take this opportunity of thanking him. That dispatch was from me as a representative of labor, and not by authority of any union or the Federated Trades Assembly. It bore my own signature.*

At a meeting of the assembly since, I state there what I did and there and in this city, no person has assailed me for that act.

Yesterday, however, I received the following communication which I will endeavor to answer, leaving out reference to legislators, or as much as possible, from a trade union or labor standpoint.

February 12, 1889. Mr. John O'Brien, President of the Federated Trades, Portland, Oregon.

Sir, I beg leave to call your attention to the fact that I have not seen nor heard of any of your unions advocating a law to protect laboring men in public works. Now is your time if you are sincere in protecting labor in all its branches, but you may not think it worthwhile to trouble yourself about the poor common laborer. I judge you so by the action of your representatives from Portland. Each and every one of them are enemies to any measure that may be introduced in either house to protect labor. The only friends of labor are Mr. Irvine, Linn County; Mr. Miller of Jackson County; and our gallant hero, Mr. Geer, Marion County. Out of the whole number, only three members are working in the interest of labor — the Portland delegation fighting against them. How is it that you are silent? Are you fools or slaves to the Oregonian? *Your dispatch to Thompson yesterday, advocating the passage of the Bull Run water bill has made enemies against labor unions. I am sorry that you should advocate such a thieving measure that would give employment to Chinese in preference to whites. Where was the provision in that thieving bill to prohibit Chinese from being employed in the construction of the Bull Run water works? Thank God we have a governor who watches those thieving bills whom each and every labor union should uphold as being the true friend of labor. Do you remember how he got the laborers paid at Corvallis? Oh no, but you select the biggest enemy to labor in the house (Thompson) to forward your dispatch to. Don't be so fast! Look ahead before you bring yourself in contempt. I hope this will (be a beginning of?) friendly (relations?) between us. As I am here, I have the advantage of favor to know our enemies and our friends. I hope you will call a special meeting of your unions in advocacy of the Irvine bill in the ___ Senate No. 61, but remember the Portland delegation are our worst enemies. Respectfully, M.H. O'Connor.*

John O'Brien's rebuttal followed:

In reply to the charge that our unions never advocated a law to protect laboring men on public works, I have only to call his attention to the report of an open meeting held February 1, 1889, in the hall of the Federated Trades. The object of the meeting was to urge legislation to protect wage earners. On page 1 of the Daily Oregonian *of February 3, a report of that meeting may be found. John M. Bower, of this city, delivered a carefully prepared address. He said, "The law should be so comprehensive as to include all the farm laborers, the kitchen servant, the sewing girl, the laborer, as well as the skilled and scientific workmen, extending the lien to machinery, etc., enumerating property subject to liens. It would make subject to a lien for 30 days, wages in preference to all other claims.*

We hope to accomplish this in the next legislature through pledges from candidates. It would cost us $300 to prepare bills to cover everything we want and we do not know how much labor it will require to bring it about, but we do not intend to make radical charges or disturb the established order of things and we hope the Multnomah delegation will respond to the support of Myers' bill to protect contractors, sub-contractors and laborers in their claims against railroad companies or ___senate trade bill No. 61.

As regards the Multnomah delegation being enemies of labor, I wish Mr. O'Connor would point out instances where any of them oppressed labor or denied its rights. The only ___ there is now on our statute of which he complains is the (lien?) law, which was framed by Hon. Joseph Simon, president of the Senate. There is not a present member of the delegation in debt to me for a vote. Inside and outside the labor unions, I cheerfully submit to the will of the majority. They are smart men of business — they know what they want and how to get it. Labor men should profit by their example. I don't intend to be discourteous to the men who represent us in Salem — who else should they dispatch to but to a member of our delegation?

In regard to being slaves to the Oregonian, that paper is being run by a solvent company. It puts out weekly to union printers over $1,000. We have nothing whatever to do with the policy of the paper. He who gives out the most work at fair wages is the greatest friend of the working men and he, who in the face of the fight changes front and goes to the rear after being so near the goal is no hero. The governor was consistent; we expected he would veto the bill.

I blame those for its defeat who made it a party measure and threw the fate of the bill into a caucus. I think it a poor way to remedy the failings of the present law on assessment and taxation by opposing bills of this character. I see no difference between $10,000 raised to build a schoolhouse or courthouse in this manner than to raise $150,000 — a sum that would do so much for the city and county as well.

Mr. O'Connor's grief over my advocating "such a thieving measure that would give employment to Chinese in preference to whites" is as devoid of truth as regards facts as is every other statement made. It is my time now to hold a stiff (reminder?). Don't be so fast! In the General Conditions for the specifications of works for the water supply for the city of Portland, I find the following:

"No Chinese or Mongolian labor will be allowed in any work enumerated in these specifications on penalty of forfeiture of the contract, at the option of the water committee."

No complaint has been handed to any of our unions from any quarter regarding the employment of Chinese. The committee, in laying nearly 30 miles of pipe, have given employment to white men. There are now employed above 50 men in this kind of work, which number will be increased next month as I am reliably informed. But this is a mere bagatello to what we have lost by reason of the failure of the bill to pass.

As to bringing myself into contempt, or those I represent, or making enemies to trade unions... What the unions have won here, they have done themselves. We owe no officeholder, save those who have sprung from the ranks, anything. We have won everything we have gained ourselves, and in our unions, local and national, is *centered all our hopes for the amelioration of the hardships of the laborer. For the support of those who patronize union labor, we are grateful. No, I cannot call a special meeting. It is not necessary. We are already pledged to such measures. I am personally acquainted with Hon. Robert Irvine. I have worked for him as a harvest hand. He treated me well, paid my wages when due... I got as good wages and treatment from his neighbors who laid no claim to be champions of labor. I am glad to learn that he is our champion, but why did you not ask me courteously, like a brother, to give the same support to that bill that I gave to the water bill. Hon. Robert Irvine has the Santiam ditch that supplies Albany water – the finest in the world running through his farm. Why did he to support an abstract, inoperative theory, purely speculative, deny the citizens of Portland, East Portland and Albina with equally good water and deprive working men the privilege of earning $1,000. He might as well, in my opinion, try to clean a field full of thistles by cutting the largest or to remedy the defects of the present assessment in voting down the Bull Run water bill. ~Captain John O'Brien*

International typographical unions throughout the U.S. and Canada were at the forefront of the movement to obtain a nine-hour workday for all trades workers. Up until then, the norm was for workers to labor 12- and even 14-hour workdays. The typographical unions went on strike in 1887, but lost out.

In the 1892 *Pacific Union Printer* biography, excerpted earlier here, it stated that, *It was during the presidency of Mr. O'Brien that all the job and weekly offices of Portland, lost in the nine-hour strike of 1887, were regained by the Union.*

Even though he was very busy with his jobs in Portland, John must have spent some time in 1888 on his farm. He was appointed the temporary postmaster of the Omro Post Office, located near his Lorane home. John's appointment began on March 26, 1888 and ended on August 8, 1888, a little over four months in length. The small post office was being consolidated with the newly-formed Lorane Post Office. Obviously, his help was needed to shut down the Omro site and help with the transition.

Back in Portland, Captain John O'Brien obviously wielded a lot of influence in the movement to give tradesmen and women a respected work environment and routine. His views on a pending strike for an eight-hour day appearing in the Sunday *Oregonian* on March 23, 1890 demonstrates this.

The *Morning Astorian* newspaper in Astoria, Oregon, carried the following headline:

"ANOTHER STRIKE... This Time it is Nearer Home"

It is estimated at present that no less than 1,500 carpenters, painters, plasterers, bricklayers, tinners, roofers, and in fact, workers of all trades, are now out of employment in this city, by reason of the lockout declared yesterday morning by the builder's union... President of the Federated Trades Union, John O'Brien, says the arrangement is not yet perfected but in the next 48 hours, a general strike will occur.

The reasons for — and the outcome of — the impending strike was described in an on-line *History of Portland, Oregon*...

When countless Chinese were recruited to provide cheap, but hard-working, labor by railroad magnates in the 1860s, Portland and San Francisco attracted the largest numbers. While they were admired for their commitment to the backbreaking work of carving out paths and laying down railroad ties, rails, and spikes, as an ethnic group, the Chinese were looked upon by whites as a threat to many livelihoods, which led to their ostracizing. A growing civil unrest and open racism followed.

Not unlike other cities, such workers as printers, typesetters, bricklayers, longshoremen, and carpenters, organized to form craft unions in the 1880s. The largest of those unions, Portland Local No. 50 of the United Brotherhood of Carpenters and Joiners, organized in September 1883, after the Northern Pacific Railroad arrived in Portland, along with another wave of Asian immigrants.

After 1890, Portland became increasingly segregated by class and ethnic district, much like other cities in America had become. That same year, two of Portland's carpenter's unions joined a national strike for the eight-hour workday, and a "closed shop" on the coattails of economic expansion, after several years of recession.

Having their demands rejected by the Portland Builders Exchange, other unions joined in the effort, holding a huge May Day rally that forced the builders back to the bargaining table and ultimately led to the settling of the strike.

John was right in the thick of it.

The Sunday Oregonian, Portland, Oregon
March 23, 1890, page 9

THE EIGHT HOUR DAY

Interview with Captain O'Brien of the Federated Trades

THE MOVEMENT ISN'T STRONG HERE

The Bricklayers Say They Are Satisfied With
Their Present Hours and Wages — Position
of the Plasterers — the Situation

The articles recently published in *The Oregonian* about the proposed eight-hour movement have excited considerable interest among the members of the various trades unions of the city, and a good many comments have been made upon them. Mr. Henry Gurr, president of the Bricklayers' union, called at the office of *The Oregonian* yesterday and gave the assurance that the union is perfectly satisfied with their present rate of $6 per day for nine-hours of work, and that no additional demand will be made.

In view of the many conflicting statements made in connection with the matter, a reporter sought an interview yesterday with Captain John O'Brien, president of the Federated Trades assembly, who is thoroughly informed on all branches of the labor situation, and adds to his wide information a disposition to harmonize all differences and help the unions to reach that point where they cannot only protect their own interests, but further those of the employer, as well. Captain O'Brien said:

"Yes, I have read the statement of Mr. Perkins in Friday's *Oregonian* of a difference between contractors and workmen, having particular reference to the carpenter work and brickwork of the new Holton House and that by reason of that difference, the contract would not be let until the matter is satisfactorily adjusted. I have seen the objections of the contractors as stated in yesterday's *Oregonian*, and saying that there will probably be trouble as the bricklayers–carpenters–plasterers, etc. have given notice that on May 1, eight hours will constitute a day's work. A well-known contractor told me that Mr. W.S. Ladd intended to erect a large building on Third and Washington, but the impending strike has caused him to lease the ground for three years for the fish market. These statements are misleading and are, to a certain extent, untrue.

"The unions placed so prominently in front as having caused the difference are almost entirely out of the fight. I saw Mr. Gurr, the president of the Bricklayer's union, a few days ago and he told me that the bricklayers had not made a demand for eight hours, but if they should do so, there would be no strike, as the unions would reduce from $6 to $5.50 for eight hours' work. The Plasterers' union have made no such demand, as that union has worked eight hours a day in this city the past seven years and, as to the carpenters, they gave notice to the contractors the 5th of last December that eight hours would constitute a day's work on or after May 1, 1890, with provision for the completion of building then contracted for to be finished on the nine-hour day. Whatever difference may arise could be settled at any time with the Brotherhood of Carpenters' and Joiners' Union—which has left the question of wages entirely out. They now receive $3 and $3.50 for nine hours. In all their notices to the Federated Trades Assembly, they stated the wages question is not to involve a strike, and before there will be a resort to a strike, a reasonable reduction undoubtedly will be conceded."

"Do you think the contractors will seek a compromise?"

"No, I do not think the contractors will make any effort to now settle the difference of wages, as they are trying to create sympathy in a dishonest way. Take, for instance, the contemplated building by Mr. Ladd. I am informed that the site requires four lots. Mr. Ladd now owns two, has a bond for a deed for another, and there is a difference of opinion between him and the owner of the fourth as to price. He thinks that the price is too high and refuses to pay it, hence the lease. Now, if that is true, I am surprised that as responsible a name as Mr. Ladd's should be used by contractors to throw all the blame on the workingman. The Holton house lot is not yet ready for the mechanics spoken of in the statement, and it probably will not be ready for that line of work until after May 1.

"The contractors' union has imposed a heavy fine on any member of their association who discharges a non-union mechanic—$150, I am told. They offer a premium, you see, for non-union men. To employ non-union men is now their main purpose and, until they make a trial of forcing union men off all their contracts, I cannot hope for peace. This is a strike of the contractors against the unions.

"I don't think they can get many non-union men here to fill the places of the union men. All the country outside is organized better than Portland, have as good or better wages, and as to the idle tradesmen in San Francisco coming here, you could not bring them here for such a purpose; they would work as laborers for $1.50 in Golden Gate Park first.

"The typographical union does not ask for a reduction of the hours of labor. Should it do so, it would reduce the scale in proportion. Personally, I think that should be the plan pursued. It was the one adopted in Australia over thirty years ago, when that country was more isolated than this was in the ox-team era. They reduce 14 per cent.

"There is a difference in climate, of course, in Australia—it is hotter and is a good reason for shorter hours, but there are trade here, as the plasterers, bricklayers, the building laborers—in fact, all the building trades—which require physical strength and endurance which is a severe strain on the system, more especially as all trades have a 'dead line' or standard of speed, as well as one of skill. Every workman has to keep his end up.

"Yes, there are points I would like to speak of, but for the present, I think a generous public will see that there are two sides to this question, and that the May day cloud is altogether too small as far as organized labor is concerned, to warrant all this abuse from the public and contractors. If the contractors wished to come to a settlement with the only union that seems to be in their way — the carpenters — I'm sure the difficulty will soon be settled satisfactorily to the trades and the public, but if the contractors mean war, as I think they do, against organized labor by the enforcement of the by-law of their association referred to, then let the responsibility rest with them, where it does as yet and will belong.

"No, I think I will not say anything in regard to statements of coercion by taking undue disadvantage, as spoken of in yesterday's *Oregonian*. The trades refer to will undoubtedly reply. In regard to the carpet baggers who think Portland finished, comment is unnecessary. I look for no strikes here May 1 so far as the unions are concerned; neither will I think for a moment that the citizens of Portland expect her trades men to work for less wages than is obtained on the Sound country or California — and let us not waste labor, but make it all productive by giving the eight-hour men a chance.

"No I don't think the responsibility lies on the workingmen for harsh statements of capitalists — they never doubt a contractor and allow their names often to be used when, if viewed from a labor standpoint, they should not. They often don't try to understand the question."

Chapter Ten

A Run For Public Office

During the late 1800s, John was not only knee-deep in union matters, he was also being considered for a Democratic nomination to run for the State Printer position to be voted on in 1890. As State Printer, he would be in charge of performing all the public printing for the State of Oregon.

On April 25, 1890, at the Democratic primary convention, Capt. John O'Brien was nominated by acclamation for the position of State Printer. His opponent, incumbent, Frank C. Baker, was a popular printer and also a consistent friend of organized labor as well.

The newspapers of the day, depending on their political affiliation, each lined up in support of its party's candidate.

The Albany Democrat: *Capt. J. O'Brien, the candidate for state printer, is highly recommended by those who know him. He will get an immense vote in Portland. (May 2, 1890)*

The Statesman Journal of Salem: *The nominee of the Democrats for state printer will be John O'Brien, a printer on the* Oregonian. *In the language of the printers, when the votes are counted, his name* will be 'pants'.[1] *The right hand man of the state printer will continue to be Frank C. Baker.* (April 24, 1890)

The Corvallis Gazette-Times: *There are two main reasons why the democratic state ticket should not be successful in June. One is that they have a mighty poor ticket, comparatively, and the other is that they have a poorer platform... The people are satisfied with Frank C. Baker for state printer. His majority will be large.* (May 2, 1890)

Being a candidate brought on more duties for the very busy man. **The Morning Astorian** newspaper reported on May 17, 1890 that *Capt. John O'Brien, president of the Federated Trades and candidate on the Democratic ticket for state printer, was in the city yesterday. He wore the blue during the civil war and marched yesterday in the ranks of the G.A.R. He returns to Portland this morning.*

```
Democratic State Ticket.

For Congress,
R. A. MILLER, of Jackson.
For Governor,
SYLVESTER PENNOYER, of Multnomah.
For Treasurer,
G. W. WEBB, of Umatilla.
For Supreme Judge,
B. F. BONHAM, of Marion.
For Secretary of State,
WM. TOWNSEND, of Lake.
For Superintendent of Public Instruction,
REV. A. LEROY, of Linn.
For State Printer,
CAPT. J. O'BRIEN, of Multnomah.
For District Attorney, 3d District,
J. J. WHITNEY, of Linn.

Joint Senator for Clackamas and Marion,
HENRY WARREN.
```

---

[1] Pants: "To inflict a crushing defeat on someone" seems to be the most logical definition I have been able to find in the Urban Dictionary. This is the verb form, but it could be equated to the use as a noun in the article.

The results of the June 1890 election were not favorable for John, but it was obvious that he was well-respected throughout the state. The vote count was 39,273 for incumbent, Frank C. Baker, and 34,125 for Capt. John O'Brien — a difference of 5,148 votes.

The loss of the election didn't mean he wouldn't be able to serve the state as a printer, however. The newly re-elected governor, Sylvester Pennoyer, appointed Capt. O'Brien as a "State printing expert" for the purpose of measuring the work done by State Printer Frank Baker.

He began traveling all over Oregon to oversee state projects involving the printing of books and other printed material, but most of his duties were based in Salem.

In an article originally printed by the *Northwest Labor Press* and quoted in the *Eugene Guard* that appeared on January 30, 1930, it was reported that when President Herbert Hoover was a young man, he used to drop into the printing office at Salem and watch Capt. O'Brien set type.

Many people don't know that when he was a young boy, Herbert Hoover, as an orphan, came to live with his uncle, Dr. Henry John Minthorn, who was the first headmaster of the Friends Pacific Academy which later became George Fox College/University in Newberg, Oregon. He was also the school superintendent at the Indian School, later "Chemawa," in neighboring Forest Grove.

While living with his uncle, "Bertie," as Hoover was fondly called, did not attend high school, but instead took night school classes to learn bookkeeping, typing and mathematics, and he attended the Friends Pacific Academy for 2½ years. He also worked in John Minthorn's Oregon Land Company office in Salem where he must have formed a friendship with Captain John O'Brien.

In August 1892, John resigned as president of the Multnomah Typographical Union #58, and was succeeded by Charles Houck.

John continued to be deeply involved in the workings of labor unions, however. In December 1892, he attended a session of the American Federation of Labor in Philadelphia as a general organizer with the group. While in Philadelphia, he was invited by the AFL to make a 4-week's lecture tour through California. His lectures covered labor questions in general and non-political trades-unionism. In addition to the tour, according to a March 23, 1893 article in the *Eugene Guard*...

He will carry on the organization of trades unions in places where they do not already flourish... Captain O'Brien was for a number of years a resident of Siuslaw precinct and still has a farm in that section.

He continued to address union meetings throughout Oregon, as well.

The year 1893 brought with it a gloomy unemployment picture. *The Morning Astorian* published an article on January 6, 1894 stating that:

Capt. J. O'Brien, of the Federated Trades, has compiled figures showing the number of unemployed in Portland. Basing the population at 80,000, he estimates that 20,000 are wage earners. Of these, sixty-three per cent are unemployed, seventeen per cent employed on full time, and twenty per cent on reduced time.

The Panic of 1893 was a serious economic depression in the United States, considered by some to be one of the worst in American history. It began in 1893 and ended in 1897, and deeply affected every sector of the economy. The unemployment rate exceeded ten percent for half a decade. It was accompanied by violent strikes and produced political upheaval that eventually led to the election of President William McKinley in 1896.

1894 was also an election year and John was once again being touted to run for State Printer. *The Morning Astorian*, on April 17, 1894, noted that there would be more competition this time at the Democratic convention.

There are so many little booms for the office of state printer that it will need a wagonload of incubators to hatch them out. I.L. Campbell, an old newspaper man, Charles Nickoll, of the Jacksonville Times; *Joseph T. Hayne of Portland, and Capt. John O'Brien, all have their friends at work, and expect to plant their separate totem poles in front of the state printers workshop.*

The Daily Capital Journal predicted that *Capt. John O'Brien would probably be named by the Democratic party for state printer.*

In an article published on February 24, 1894, the newspaper elaborated on its prediction.

Capt. O'Brien is said to be lying in wait for the Democratic nomination of state printer. He is Pennoyer's expert who passes on all the state printing bills and measures up all the thousands of dollars worth of work that is performed by the Republican state printer. Being a Democrat and a labor man, he has had the scrutiny of all the work done in the office the past eight years and knows just what there is in it. He will make a strong pull for the place.

When the Democratic convention, held in Astoria, rolled around on April 17, Capt. John O'Brien had been unanimously elected to carry the banner for the Democratic party in the general election for the state printer race. But, when the election was held, the results were not in John's favor. His Republican counterpart, W.H. Leeds had won with 40,957 votes in a four-man race. Capt. John O'Brien came in third with 19,991. The other two candidates were William "Doc" Orton, who was supported by Frank Baker to be his Republican successor, with 23,211, and McKibben with 2,138 votes.

Chapter Eleven

Spreading His Wings to *The Sun*

In June 1894, true to his dedication to ensuring jobs for the working man, Capt. John O'Brien, along with four partners, George Pope, Benton Killin, W.F. Osburn and E.D. McKee, formed The Sun Publishing Company of Portland. In an article published by the *Medford Mail*, it states: *The company proposes to publish daily, weekly, and Sunday newspapers. The capital stock is $35,000, divided into 3,500 shares. This is the paper that will possibly be started by the typesetters recently thrown out of employment in the* Oregonian *office by the introduction of typesetting machinery.*

By October 1894, the Sun Publishing group founded a newspaper called the *Portland Daily Sun*... or simply, *THE SUN*.

An article in the *St. Helens Mist* newspaper, dated October 12, 1894, tells a bit about it.

Portland's new daily and Sunday newspaper will make its first appearance next Monday morning. The Sun *will be the name of the new publication, and its manager will be Capt. John O'Brien. The Sun will cast its rays of light upon the people of Portland and the adjacent country and make all opposition to democratic principles wilt under the penetrating arguments cast from* The Sun's *fountain of light.* The Mist *will cheerfully comply with the manager's request, by postal, to exchange.*

The first issue was indeed published on Monday, October 14, 1894. The masthead on the editorial page doesn't list any of the editorial staff, so I'm not sure if any of the editorials were written by Captain John, but I imagine that besides manager, he oversaw the printing aspect of the production of the paper. It wouldn't surprise me, however, if he did add editorial comment occasionally.

Fortunately, I was able to find microforms of *The Sun* at the Knight Library at the University of Oregon. As I began to scan them, I found myself focusing mainly on the editorial pages. The first editorial was titled "Our Greeting."

This is the first issue of THE SUN. *It will be published every day of the year by* THE SUN PUBLISHING COMPANY. *Composed, as the company is, of many stockholders,* THE SUN *could hardly be otherwise than independent in politics. It will uphold the true business interests of the city, state and tributary territory. It will endeavor to induce desirable immigration of capital, whether it be represented by money, or by labor, holding that every industrious citizen adds wealth and increased prosperity. It will urge the best of all co-measures for the city and state, and never will it for any purpose whatever misrepresent any of the actual conditions, whether of city or country, whose mutual dependence is of paramount value to each.*

THE SUN's *business is to give the news; however it will do that will appear from day to day. That with increasing revenues it will improve its general newsgathering facilities may be accepted as a wise business proposition. After all, what one most desires is home news, and in the matter of local news,* THE SUN *will be thorough and comprehensive.*

The Sun

Issued every morning, by The Sun Publishing Company, at 162-164 Second street.

DELIVERED BY CARRIER:

Per week (including Sunday)..........15 cents
Per month (including Sunday).........65 cents
Single copies .... 5 cents

BY MAIL, INCLUDING POSTAGE:

One year (including Sunday)........ $ 7 00
Six months (including Sunday)......... 3 50

If our friends who favor us with manuscripts for publication wish to have rejected articles returned, they must in all cases send stamps for that purpose.

All communications intended for the Editorial department, should be addressed, "Editor of the Sun," Portland, Or.

All communications of a business nature should be addressed,

THE SUN, Portland, Or.

The people's welfare is protected as much by competition in news as it is by competition of railroads, and THE SUN *being devoted to the common good, its expressions will always be found fearless and honest in the cause of good government, national, state and municipal.*

To our patrons, we desire to say that the expensive details of the publication of a paper of this size is reduced to a minimum of cost by reason of its cooperative character. Every person, from the editorial force down to the newsboy who will deliver it to the readers, is enlisted in the cause and its success.

The price places it at the command of all classes of our people, and its popularity is already evidenced by a large list of volunteer subscribers, who have our thanks for this manifestation of their appreciation and confidence.

With antagonism to none, and hearty good wishes to all, THE SUN *has been started.*

As soon as the first issue was published, it was obvious that there was a lot of support and respect for it among not only the increasing number of subscribers, but newspaper editors all over Oregon.

- *Portland's new daily newspaper,* THE SUN, *is out and a sparkling, six-column quarto it is, too.* Salem Statesman
- *The first issue of the* Portland Sun *is at hand. It presents the best appearance of any paper that has entered the field against the Oregonian. Its telegraphic service is a good one and its local department is complete. It is independent. May it shine successfully.* Albany Democrat
- *The first copy of the* Daily Morning Sun *of Portland was issued this morning. It has a fair telegraphic service, is well edited and is typographically neat in appearance. It is printed on the cooperative plan and is independent in politics. We wish the promoters of the new venture success.* Eugene Guard
- The Daily Sun *came out yesterday with a bright appearance and a good deal of news. Its promoters are a body of printers working on the cooperative plan. The* Oregonian *notes its advent as a commendable enterprise , and hopes it will do well. There is ample room in Oregon for new undertakings in almost any line of effort. The future is always in the hands of those who work for it.* Morning Oregonian
- *There is certainly room in Portland for two good dailies and we hope* THE SUN *may exist and prosper for all time.* – Valley Transcript, Dallas, Oregon
- THE SUN *is run by union printers on the cooperative plan, and with the usual energy displayed by members of the craft, should do well. The* Astorian *wishes them success.* Daily Astorian
- THE SUN *gives evidence of being in the hands of thorough newspaper men and its typographical appearance leaves no doubt as to the character of the labor employed.* Tacoma Morning Union

- *THE SUN, of Portland, has made its appearance. It is a neat and newsy eight-page morning paper and takes dispatches from the Eastern Associated Press. THE SUN should have started out with a better showing of advertisements.* Astoria Daily Budget
- *THE SUN is getting a hustle on. The first issue gave an account of the robbery here, and today it comes out with the full decision of the Supreme Court in the branch asylum case. It is right in the swim, and will make the older papers get a move on for state news, or else get left.* The Dalles Chronicle
- *THE SUN is a bright newsy sheet, and will in time become one of the leading papers of the state.* La Grande Gazette
- *It is independent from a political standpoint and will labor for the best interests of the state in general.* Baker City Blade
- *It is a model in typographical neatness and print, and is full of all the latest news — telegraphic, local and otherwise.* Condon Globe
- *A pleasing thing about the sheet is that it gives fairly complete Puget Sound and especially Seattle news, a thing which no paper has heretofore done.* Eugene State Journal
- *The first number contained a big telegraphic scoop on the Oregonian, and it bids fair to give the big daily a stiff competition. THE SUN is to be independent in politics.* Oregon City Enterprise
- *It certainly is a credible production for a beginning, and all the harm we wish it is success. To fill the bill, it must be aggressive and fearless, never cringing to anyone.* Troutdale Champion
- *It is a credit to the metropolis, being ably edited, neat in looks and filled with the latest news. The Times hopes that it will be liberally sustained, as it well deserves success.* Jacksonville Times

- *Judging from present appearances,* THE SUN *will be a neatly issued paper and well filled with news and is here to stay. The merchants of Portland are quite well represented, but not so much as we should expect.* Gervais Star
- *We welcome* THE SUN; *it is needed. Portland needs it; the people need it; and if it will continue to shine, and we believe it will, its influence will be felt and its power for good acknowledged and appreciated.* Eastern Oregonian
- *It seems to take with the Vancouver people, many of whom are getting tired of the one-sided news reports from this city and the cold-shoulder manner in which we are being treated. Morning Sun, we greet you and may you shine long and brightly.* Vancouver (Wash) Columbian
- *The new paper is ably edited in all its departments with telegraphic correspondence from all parts of the Northwest and Eastern Associated Press dispatches from all parts of the world. No paper ever started in Portland under such flattering prospects, and we predict for it abundant success under its experienced management.* Hood River Glacier
- *"Have you seen the new paper?" has been on the lips of everybody during the week. And the response invariably has been, "I have." It seems that everybody has seen it and everybody has subscribed. In three days, their books revealed a subscription list of 4,000 names. What is best of all, we get what now is 65 cents a month what has cost $1.80 heretofore, and not so good.* Portland (Or) Frater

The Sun had an impressive beginning. Their October 23, 1894 issue included an apology to its readers for delays in getting the papers out on time. *The company and the public could not have anticipated the phenomenal rush of subscribers and the rapid rise in circulation.*

At the beginning of the second week of operation, it was claiming upwards of 5,000 subscribers and a rate of 300 new subscribers coming on board each day. New personnel for the business office and distribution center were being hired, and a new press with the capabilities of keeping up with the huge demands was ordered.

I thought it strange that when researching the paper, before I discovered the microforms at the University of Oregon, I found little mention of it except for a few pieces in small town newspapers. There was nothing that I was able to find in the Oregonian until the short-lived welcome piece from the *Morning Oregonian* that I included in the previous list. After scanning the first reel in the microform department, I found out why. The reason was contained in another editorial.

Soon after *The Sun*'s inception, the two Portland dailies were at war. The main crux of the disagreement seems to have been based on the controversial gold monetary standard supported by the *Oregonian* vs the bi-metalism double standard backed by *The Sun*.

In the November 11, 1864 issue of *The Sun*, there were two editorials lambasting the *Oregonian*. I doubt that the editorials were written by John O'Brien, because he was known to be a bit more diplomatic in his writing style than the person who wrote these pieces.

The first editorial called "The *Oregonian*'s Inconsistency," focuses on the glaring differences the two papers had on the brewing economic controversy of the time.

...Nevertheless, our contemporary must fear this small class of our citizens (those who support the double standard), *possibly because they are as yet unconfined in any of our institutions of restraint, as it took sufficient of its time and its valuable space in its yesterday's issue to attack, attempt to ridicule and threaten the advocates of the double standard in seven different editorials. Somebody is evidently alarmed.*

An editorial just below that one was titled, "A Coward's Resort" in which *The Sun* openly chastises the *Oregonian* for indirectly criticizing *The Sun* behind its back.

The Oregonian, *in pursuance of its accustomed policy of arrogant and dictatorial domination — of assuming superiority to everything and everybody in this country — goes up to Eastern Oregon to quote something with which to reply to* The Sun. *It will not mention this paper, which fact* The Sun *can afford to ignore, since, within a month and laboring under difficulties that have vexed and alienated many of its friends* and subscribers, *it has obtained a larger circulation than its contemporary. We do not need that paper's notice; in fact, any favorable notice would, evidently, be detrimental to* The Sun.

But this method of attempting to reply to the arguments of this paper by indirection – by quoting somebody else – by such studied and visible contortions – is amusing. Only a coward resorts to such method; and a bully is generally a coward...

The gauntlet had been thrown... in a very public way.

...Truth, vigor, prescience, fidelity, unselfishness, fearlessness, perseverance – only these qualities will make a daily paper in a large city a permanent success. All these require brain, industry, courage, and above all – for without it, all these must break down – money.

Whether the present enterprise will develope (sp) *these qualities remains to be seen – for their development is necessarily a matter of gradual growth. But, if not now, some time before very long, such a paper will appear in Portland and will stay. It is this sort of paper for which there is a "field" and a "want."*

This was the editorial published in the October 22, 1864, issue of *The Sun*. The acceptance and visions of the fledgling newspaper seemed sound. There seemed to be a large support base for another daily newspaper in Portland to rival the *Oregonian*.

Although I have been unable to find out what happened to make *The Sun* shut its doors in less than a year, I assume that the last criteria about which the editorial of October 22 spoke was the reason for its demise—money, or the lack thereof.

It very possibly could have something do with the strong stand the paper took against those who supported the gold standard... "the money-lending class," according to *The Sun*'s editors in an editorial published in the July 31, 1895 newspaper.

...Why should the opinions of the money-lending class be accepted without question by governments? Can it be doubted that any system they may have the opportunity of recommending will contain some element designed to advance their own interests?...

That editorial appeared just one day before a boldly-placed advertisement called "A Special Notice" was positioned in the upper left-hand corner of the front page of the August 1, 1895 issue.

Owing to certain circumstances, The Sun *force has "taken a tumble" and refused to work last night. For nearly 10 months the men have struggled to give the people an acceptable paper. It may not yet be too late to redeem it to its usefulness. Whatever is done must be done immediately. Will the businessmen and interested parties come to the rescue or do they prefer to be dictated to and governed by ring* (ring = "individuals engaged in improper or unlawful activities" - *Miriam Webster Dictionary) and 10-cent politicians? If they choose the latter, vale* (farewell) Sun, *vale Portland, vale freedom in the Northwest. Quien Sabe?* (Who knows?)

To call attention to their notice and plight, the "*Sun*" portion of the flag — the logo — at the top of the page was upside down as were ads and graphics on the inside pages — one of them for *The Weekly Sun*'s subscription rates. It didn't say, but I assume that *The Weekly Sun* was meant to continue.

The last issue of *The Sun* was published on August 3, 1895. Curiously, in a small note placed next to the flag, is written: **The Sun Shines:** The Portland Daily SUN *will shine on many graves of people now alive.*

The rest of the issue was printed normally without any indication that *The Sun* had sunk below the horizon.

Chapter Twelve

Wending His Way Towards Retirement

About the time that the newspaper folded, John began spending more and more time at his farm in Lorane.

In his pension application, John wrote that he moved permanently back to Lorane and his beloved homestead in April 1895. He and his wife, Julia, had a home in Portland at 374 Sixth Street, as well. John stayed at the Portland home while in the city since he was still active with his newspaper into August, his union work in Portland, and his speaking tours from all indications.

It's known that Julia preferred city life to that of the country and she continued to make Portland her permanent home, but spent time with John on the farm whenever possible.

In fact, a visit to Lorane was reported in the *Cottage Grove Echo-Leader*:

Capt. O'Brien, one of the best practical printers in Oregon, and late manager of the Portland Sun, made the Echo-Leader a pleasant call on Monday. He has gone to his ranch on Siuslaw, and will take two months vacation, where the fresh mountain air and pure spring water will give a grand appetite.

One of the meetings of representatives from various trade unions, held on April 14, 1899, that John attended in Salem was held to discuss the possibility of forming a Federated Trade Assembly in the Salem area. John was asked to address the group and the *Daily Capital Journal* covered the talk.

Capt. O'Brien was called on and gave a short informal talk, his idea being, in part, that the only way for the laborer to get strength enough to accomplish anything is to organize; that, so far, the skilled laborers are the only ones who seem to thoroughly understand this, but farmers and others are beginning to see it more clearly. All through the hard times, wages were kept up wherever there were good labor unions. The early closing movement in Salem is a good thing and this federation, if perfected, will help to make it permanent. People are studying political economy more than ever before and this has grown out of the labor unions.

It will only be a little while before the masses of the people will be better educated on these questions than ever before. Education is the great civilizing and equalizing agent of today, as gunpowder was, when first used. Gunpowder destroyed the old system of feudal slavery by destroying the supremacy of the mailed knight.

The Captain drew a lesson of encouragement from his experience during the civil war. On many occasions, an easy victory could have been won with little delay or loss if the army had known just how badly rattled the enemy were. He spoke of the label system as one of the most effective weapons in the hands of organized labor.

In 1900, John made a point of entering apples grown in his Lorane orchard in the annual Lorane Fair. He won first prize for his apple display.

John was a much sought-after speaker. Even when he was regenerating at his Lorane homestead, John was asked to talk. In December 1901, he had spent Thanksgiving in Lorane and the event was written up in the community column of the *Eugene Guard* newspaper:

We had a very nice time here Thanksgiving. Capt. Jno. O'Brien made a very interesting address...

John took an interest in the Lane County Democratic Party during this time, as well. Along with S.G. Lockwood and Hiram

LORANE'S FAIR.

The following completed list of premiums and prize-winners at the Lorane Agricultural Society Fair will be read with interest. It came too late for publication with the writeup of last week, but will be none the less appreciated now:

General exhibit—
1st prize, $5 .... William N Crow
2d prize, $2.50 .... R Crow

Grain and grasses—
1st prize, Daily Oregonian... C E Russell
2d prize, Weekly Oregonian...J H Crow

Pieced quilt—
1st prize, Sunday Oregonian. Mrs J Crow

House plants—
1st prize, Ladies' Home Journal
.... Mrs M L Tompkins
2d prize, $1 .... Mrs C M Cowan

Apple jelly—
1st prize, The Household. Mrs J Atkinson

Blackberry jelly—
1st prize, 50c .... Mrs J Atkinson

Homemade rug—
1st prize, Eugene Guard..... Mrs H Pipes

Potato exhibit—
1st prize, Pacific Homestead...N J Crow

Light bread—
1st prize, Eugene Register... Mrs J Settle

Tomato exhibit—
1st prize, The Leader..... Mrs C M Cowan

Apple exhibit—
1st prize, Bohemia Nugget..........
.... Capt John O'Brien

Canned fruit—
1st prize, Weekly Oregonian...
.... Mrs C M Cowan

Butter—
1st prize, A lovely glass set.........
.... Miss Jennette Davidson
2d prize, 50c .... Mrs C E Russell

Five largest potatoes—
1st prize, 50c .... C F Zilkey

Pumpkin pie—
1st prize, 50c .... Mrs S J Doty

Custard pie—
1st prize, 50c .... Mrs J H Crow

Hemstitched handkerchief—
1st prize, fancy clock, Mrs Doak Zumwalt

Plymouth Rock chickens—
1st prize, 50c .... J H Crow

Minoccas chicks—
1st prize, 50c .... W N Crow

Bantam chicks—
1st prize, 50c .... L E Ward

Polled Durham Bull—
1st prize, 50c .... J W Crow

Fancy work—First prizes—
Knit lace collection .... Mrs C M Cowan
Pin cushion .... Mrs Ben Lee
Shell flowers .... Mrs D Slagle
Crotchet matts... .... Miss Norma Doty
Embroidered doilies...Miss M Lockwood
Picture throw......... Mrs Charles Wiltse
Sofa throw................. Miss Knoop
Sofa pillars .... Mrs L E Ward
Oil paintings......... Mrs M L Tompkins
Battenburg doilies......... Mrs A Rogers
Patchwork by 8-year-old girl......
.... Miss Alice Wheeler
Work bag......... Miss Norma Doty
Bureau scarf.................. Mrs Ben Lee
Mosaic quilt......... Miss Cassie Cowan
Fancy quilt............... Mrs J Atkinson
Patchwork quilt of 800 pieces......
.... Miss Ida Kelly
Drawn rug .... Mrs Charles Lott
Pieced rug............... Mrs Charles Conant

Flowers—
Cut flowers and roses. Mrs G B Standish
Sweet peas............ Mrs Thos Richardson
Tea roses......... .... Mrs Elliot
Dahlias .... Mrs W N Crow

Garden—
A B Gilbert, M Railsback, J W Hicks, Mr Davidson and J H Crow each had a fine exhibit of garden truck, and Mrs S G Lockwood a fine exhibit of monstrous peppers.

L E Ward exhibited a gourd 4½ feet long.

S H McKernan received first prize on shingles and John Settle first prize on shakes.

James Hemenway received first prize on ores from Bohemia and Hildred Inman first prize on ores from Southern Oregon.

C E Russell exhibited a handmade knife 200 years old.

Mrs Tompkins and J W Hicks exhibited curios from Manilla and Chicamagua.

Quite a number of exhibits were taken away before the secretary secured the list.

An October 26, 1900 article in the Cottage Grove *Bohemia Nugget* showing John the winner in the apple category, sponsored by the *Bohemia Nugget*

Wingard, he was chosen as a delegate during the Lane County Democratic Convention in 1902.

In 1903, the Federated Trades Assembly of Portland was not popular with those working to establish the Lewis and Clark Exposition to be held in Portland in 1905. An article appeared in the *Camas Prairie Chronicle* of Cottonwood, Idaho lamenting the position the Federated Trades of Portland had taken:

In declaring its purpose to defeat by referendum vote, if possible, the state appropriation of $600,000 for the Lewis and Clark Exposition of 1905, the federal trades assembly of Portland has dealt what now appears to be a death blow to the fair project. The directors of the fair held a conference this afternoon behind closed doors and decided to stop all work of preparation and all expenditures of money pending determination of the referendum matter. If the state appropriation shall be defeated on referendum vote, then suspension of the work ordered today will be made permanent. If the action of the legislature shall be sustained by the people, work will be resumed.

The resolutions of the federated trades council says that property owners have raised rents, sawmills have raised the price of lumber and have not raised wages, painters and carpenters have been refused an advance in pay, the cost of living generally has increased, and as the fair, as they conceive, will be a detriment to the working man, they call on organized labor to set its ban of disapproval on the project.

A referendum vote failed to materialize, however, and the Lewis and Clark Centennial Exposition was held, as scheduled, in 1905. The exposition attracted both exhibits and visitors from around the world. During the exposition's four-month run, it attracted over 1.6 million visitors, and featured exhibits from 21 countries. Portland grew from 161,000 to 270,000 residents between 1905 and 1910, a spurt that has been attributed to the exposition.

Initiative, Referendum and Recall

Through his affiliation with the Federated Trades Assembly, Capt. John O'Brien became acquainted with William Simon U'Ren, known as "Referendum U'Ren" for his single-minded devotion to developing an Initiative and Referendum system in Oregon. His dream was to allow Oregon citizens to directly initiate amendments to the Oregon State Constitution, as well as enact new state statutes. He also felt that Oregon citizens should have a voice in overturning statutes or laws passed by the Oregon legislature in a process called referendum.

U'Ren had been forced in 1892 to give up his law practice as a result of an asthma attack and, having no family in the area, he was nursed back to health by the Lewelling family, prominent local fruit growers who shared his dream. Seth Lewelling,[1] in particular, worked closely alongside U'Ren.

It's possible that John was one of the committee of 17 that made up the Oregon Direct Legislation League in 1897. It consisted of representatives of the Oregon Farmer's Alliance, labor unions, bankers, the state bar association, and editor of the Portland Oregonian, Harvey W. Scott, brother of suffragette, Abigail Scott Duniway.

In 1903, John, as the president of the Federated Trades Assembly, was one of a committee of organized labor formed by U'Ren, to draft amendments to the landmark ballot measure that had been passed in 1902 by the voters.

According to an issue of Samuel Gompers' *American Federalist* magazine, dated July 1912:

They (the committee) *met in the Llewellyn (sp) cabin on his Milwaukee homestead and there drafted the Initiative and Referendum amendments, also the little pamphlets they sent out to the voters of Oregon. One of the wild dreams of the little group was to issue a State pamphlet at the expense of the whole people for the presentation of arguments for and against any Initiative or Referendum measure... This dream, therefore, has become a reality.*

So, it appears that Captain John O'Brien had a direct hand in today's use of voter's pamphlets for each major election, as well.

State and union issues weren't the only things that interested John. Even when he went to Lorane to take a break from the big city, he became involved in lending his voice for the improvement of his community, too.

---

1   Seth Lewelling is known to have developed the Bing cherry in the family's orchards located near Milwaukee, Oregon

On October 3, 1903, the *Eugene Guard* published an article from the *Cottage Grove Leader*...

Capt. O'Brien of the upper Siuslaw country, was in town Saturday agitating the connection of the Lorane-Cottage Grove wagon road with the Florence road, which will only require the construction of about three miles of road. Mound, Conner and Prairie precincts have contributed $270 for this purpose and the county court has provided $100. A construction crew is, at present, pushing work on the road which when the connection is made will be a great convenience to South Lane County as well as Florence and the coast section. It will give Cottage Grove and Lorane a direct route to the coast and turn some of the traffic this way, all of which goes to Eugene at the present time.

Julia spent her time after raising their family in charity work, apparently. Her name wasn't in the news nearly as much as John's, but she obviously gave of herself to her church and other organizations that she had a special interest in.

The February 27, 1904 issue of the *Oregon Daily Journal* reported an upcoming fair that was being planned to help raise money to liquidate some outstanding debts accumulated by St. Michael's Catholic Church in Portland. According to the article, Mrs. John O'Brien worked with the "A.O.H," or Ancient Order of Hibernians, an Irish Catholic fraternal organization whose members must be Catholic and either born in Ireland or of Irish descent.

Chapter Thirteen

Home At Last

At the age of 67, John decided that it was time to retire from his union work in Portland and the need to truly make the Lorane farm his permanent home was strong. I can only imagine that he was extremely tired, and the balm that the farm offered him each time he returned was something that he longed for on a permanent basis.

He would no longer have to frequently board the train to make the trip to Portland to put out fires and work on legislation for the union. He could spend his days working his land. So, in 1907, he came home to stay.

John O'Brien started his retirement out with a bang... or perhaps the event is why he decided to pick that particular time in 1907 to retire to a home that was left empty too much of the time.

An interesting newspaper article appeared in *Eugene Register* on April 12, 1907. It's unclear if John and Julia were present at the time or not, but it brought some excitement to the area.

Bandit Left Blood Trail; Fenwick Fought Him in Cabin; Shot Through Coat

In parrying blows, Fenwick's arm bruised — trailed into Douglas County

L.E. Ward, who resides three miles south of Lorane was in Eugene yesterday and called at the Register office to inform us about the bandit with whom Mel Fenwick had a hand-to-hand encounter Wednesday morning in the Gibson cabin.

The story given by the Register on Thursday morning was, in the main, correct, except Fenwick received no wound but was shot through the coat and had his arm bruised, parrying the blows.

The story of the battle as told (by) Mr. Ward is as follows:

Fenwick went to Capt. O'Brien's with his wife to stay several days in order to be near several cabins that the bandit had been making his headquarters. Some of the Lorane people thought that after having been fired at during the previous encounter, the fellow would leave, but Fenwick did not think so and his surmise was correct.

On Thursday night at the Gray home, the bandit was driven away from the smoke house by Mr. Gray who fired a number of shots at him.

Wednesday morning at about 10:00 o'clock, Fenwick went to the Gibson cabin which the fellow had occupied before, and opened the door. As he did so, the bandit with revolver in hand met him and attempted to fire. The revolver clicked twice but did not go off.

Owing to the darkness in the cabin, Fenwick could not see his antagonist and was at a disadvantage. He leaped inside the cabin and a hand-to-hand encounter followed, the criminal firing three shots at Fenwick, one of which ploughed its way through his coat. Fenwick fired several shots with his rifle, the last one bringing a yell from his antagonist who fell to the floor. Thinking he had mortally wounded the bandit, and fearing he had a confederate close by, Fenwick left the cabin and went a half mile to the nearest house and notified Hardy Crow, who has been deputized by Sheriff Fisk to arrest the bandit, of what had taken place. When Crow and a crowd of farmers arrived, they went to the cabin. They found blood-soaked blankets on the floor where the bandit had lain for some time, pieces of cloth, blood-soaked and lying about showed that he had made bandages to stanch the flow of blood.

The window was open, and on the sill there was plenty of blood where the bandit had crawled through. They followed his trail for half a mile by the blood; at one place a log on which he sat decorated with carmine.

Two posses were formed, one of 8 men and another of 12. They scoured the woods as best they could that night.

A message last evening from W.W. Jackson, the Lorane merchant, who was one of the members of the posse, said that both crowds had returned without finding their man and it is the firm belief that he has got a confederate who has got him out of the way. They succeeded in trailing him to the Douglas County line and are satisfied he traveled down the coast in Douglas.

Mr. Ward says that Lorane people for miles around have been terrorized by this fellow who lived by entering the houses and appropriating what he wanted to eat and as a result, the housewives are afraid to stay at home alone.

Nothing has occasioned so much excitement among Lane's rural population for a long time as the daring depradations of this strange character who has infested the Lorane country since before Christmas.

That he is a bad one is beyond question of a doubt and if not seriously injured, he will very likely make trouble for Douglas residents or if perhaps crazy, return to his old haunts to add fresh chapters to the startling episode.

I get the impression that when this story was written, John was not yet retired and was not at home at the time, but it gives an interesting account of his neighbors and how they helped each other in times of peril.

At the time that the 1910 census was taken, John was listed in Lorane with his son, 40-year-old William F. O'Brien. Census and newspaper accounts show that he was seldom alone. Frequently his wife, son or one of their daughters came to stay with him for varying amounts of time.

That same census page also showed the names of some of his neighbors in the Siuslaw Precinct—Edgar and William R. Kelly, John Humphreys, Richard Crow, Aaron Gilbert, James Chapman, Charles Simpson, Arthur Hileman, Jacob Runk, Cynthia Landreth, George Farman, Eve Sharp and Herbert Doty and their families.

Never one to kick back and let life pass him by, John took part in his community. He belonged to the Lorane Grange #54 and the Eugene Masonic Lodge #11, and in the 1910 elections, was chosen as the "first clerk" along with E.S. Addison and Irving Petrie for the Siuslaw precinct. The appointed judges for the election were W.B. Stone, E.E. Farman and W.C. Billings.

A September 22, 1911 article in the *Cottage Grove Sentinel* contained a small blurb at the bottom of its front page about John O'Brien:

Capt. O'Brien, who has a ranch on the Siuslaw below Lorane, has one of the largest apple crops in this section of Oregon. The captain "smudged" when there were frosts and, as a result, has a bumper crop of fine fruit.

On December 26, 1912, the same *Cottage Grove Sentinel* published a front-page article on John:

Veteran of Civil War, Aged 72
Runs Siuslaw Farm Unaided

Captain John O'Brien, Still Hale, Hearty and Erect, Is an Unique Character of the Lorane Country

Living alone on his 160-acre ranch a few miles from Lorane in the Siuslaw Valley, Capt. John O'Brien, a veteran of the civil war, 72 years of age and hale and hearty, does his own farm work and harvests his own crops, disdaining the assistance of neighbors. This fall he harvested 125 bushels of potatoes and a cellar of apples.

The doughty captain does not look his age. His blue eyes are still clear, he is only partially bald and he wears a full military beard, slightly gray. His appetite is in keeping with his activities. For Thanksgiving dinner, he cooked himself two full-size roosters.

The captain has a wife, a son and four daughters, but they live in Portland, Mrs. O'Brien spending summer months on the ranch, when the commissary department is turned over to her.

Mr. O'Brien was born September 18, 1840, in the province of Connaught, Ireland. He landed in New York with his parents the Sunday before Christmas in the year 1847, at 6 years of age. He spent his younger years in Connecticut, entering a New Haven printing office as apprentice at 16 and working at that trade until the news of the fall of Fort Sumpter. That night, he and a number of friends rushed to the armory to join the so-called 90 days picnic and enlisted in 1st regiment Connecticut Volunteers, Heavy Artillery. His regiment was one of those sent to the Potomac to capture Richmond. He was promoted regularly until when mustered out September 25, 1865, one week after his 25th anniversary, he had risen to the rank of captain. His regiment was engaged in hand-to-hand conflicts at Hannibal Court House and White Oak Swamp in June 1862, and had a similar experience at Fort Stedman in March 1865.

After the war, the captain moved to Montana and in 1872, came to Oregon and took a soldier's homestead on the land which he now occupies. His faculties are still clear and he serves as school clerk and justice of the peace but speaks with reluctance of his war time experiences.

Capt. O'Brien wasn't a recluse. He enjoyed people, as did his wife, Julia. Julia loved the children of Lorane. All of the

Julia O'Brien at the Lorane farm

neighborhood children knew that they would be treated to a large white mug of milk and a sugar cookie whenever they stopped by while she was there. Later, her daughter, Katie, carried on the same tradition.

John was known to be a kind, gentle man. He was always able to find work for anyone who was in need of a job, and to show how respected he was in the area, many turned to him for advice of all kinds.

One of the stories told about him while in Lorane was that he is credited with saving Everett Runk's life. Mrs. Runk lost several babies after giving birth to them. When she delivered her son, Everett, Captain O'Brien suggested that she feed him goat's milk instead of nursing him. She followed his advice and Everett grew to adulthood. Both Mrs. Runk and Captain O'Brien always felt that was due to his good advice.

Another piece of advice given by Captain O'Brien for which he is remembered was when he suggested to a neighbor, Stephen Gilbert, that he could heal the boils in his daughter Edna's ear by blowing cigar smoke into the affected ear and placing cotton in it to hold the smoke inside. It apparently worked, because it is said that by the next morning the boil had broken and was in the process of healing.

The large home that John built for his family before they moved to Siuslaw in 1872, sat on the 160 acres he obtained through the Homestead Act. A small creek, called Letz Creek, that flowed into the nearby headwaters of the Siuslaw River, ran through their property. At one time, there was a small covered bridge that spanned it on the road still called Letz Creek Road that passes through the property, today.

There was a small patch of land close to the Siuslaw River which they called the Five Cent Patch. The few remaining Native Americans in the area once had a sweat house there where, in the winter, they took steam baths and then jumped into the icy river. There were also three Indian graves believed to be on the Five Cent Patch, too.

Katie O'Brien Gilbert, one of John and Julia's daughters, remembered that there were still a few Native Americans left in the area when she was a child. She recalled finding numerous strings of native beads and many arrowheads on the property.

That, and several other stories about John O'Brien's early years in Lorane, were told to me by Rena Gilbert Gowing, a grandniece of John's daughter, Katie. It was said that during the first winter they lived on their Lorane farm, Captain John O'Brien bought hay in Lorane (It was then called "Siuslaw"), and carried it on his back to his home five miles away to feed a cow so that it would produce milk for his ailing infant daughter.

He preferred walking and did a lot of it. On one trip home from Lorane, when he was carrying a jar of fresh milk and some fresh meat that a neighbor must have given him, a cougar followed him all the way home.

In later years, Captain O'Brien made the trip into Lorane each month, usually with Frank Gilbert who worked for him. They rode in Gilbert's wagon to cash John's Civil War pension check and to buy supplies at the Jackson/Addison Store.

Sometime in 1912, a notice was placed in the *Cottage Grove Leader*:

Capt. John O'Brien of the Siuslaw section, was in town yesterday to take the 10 o'clock train for Portland for a business trip. We had a very pleasant visit with Mr. O'Brien in the evening as he returned from the city. Mr. O'Brien is a newspaperman of broad experience, having held good positions on the large city dailies of Portland and San Francisco. But, for some years, has chosen life of the farmer instead.

The 1920 U.S. Census, taken on January 8 in the Siuslaw Precinct, shows both John and Julia living at the farm. Despite his advancing age—he was 80 years old in 1920—he was obviously staying physically active. Another notice in the October 14, 1922 Eugene, *Morning Register*, under its "Letts Creek News Notes" section, mentions that *Capt. O'Brien has been hauling flooring from the Addison Mill. He is planning on putting a new floor in his house.*

He was obviously a well-liked and respected member of the Lane County community, and his comings and goings were frequently recorded in several area papers.

Descendant, John Dwyer, made an interesting observation, too.

In 1926, (silent movie star) Buster Keaton, brought his production team to Cottage Grove to film the Civil War-inspired motion picture "The General." A business holiday was declared for the day that the climactic train wreck was to be filmed and the entire town turned out to watch this spectacular event. John, or "Captain Jack," as he was affectionately known, likely shared some of the celebrity status on such a day.

John was 88 years of age when Julia and one of his daughters, Nellie O'Brien True, stopped by on their way home to Portland from where they had been visiting in Los Angeles, California. *Mrs. O'Brien is visiting her husband in Lorane. Mrs. True and children have gone on to Seattle, Washington where they will make their future home.* This was reported in the July 18, 1828 edition of the *Eugene Guard*.

Buster Keaton in scene from "The General" with a mortar.
http://www.doctormacro.com

Another "The General" scene. Courtesy of Curtis Irish

Ten days later, on July 28, 1828, *Mrs. John O'Brien and daughter, Mrs. Katie Hannigan, who are visiting with Capt. O'Brien, down the Siuslaw, have gone to Portland to spend a few days*, as reported by the *Morning Register*.

Their daughter Katie O'Brien Hannigan, who was widowed in 1921, began spending more and more time with John in order to take care of her aged father.

A news note that appeared in the *Eugene Guard* on February 22, 1929:

Mrs. Katie Hannigan, who is spending the winter with her father, Capt. John O'Brien of Lorane, was called to Seattle Thursday by the illness of her daughter.

Katie was soon living full time with John and it must have meant a great deal to him to be able to spend his remaining days on his beloved farm.

On January 20, 1930, John was the subject of another article on his life. This one appeared earlier in the *Oregon Labor Press* magazine and was quoted in the *Eugene Guard*.

Captain O'Brien, 92, Is Given Write-up

Captain John O'Brien, 92 year old farmer living near Lorane, is given a lengthy write-up in the last issue of the Oregon Labor Press. *He is an ex-employee of the* Oregonian *composing room. Captain O'Brien was born in Ireland in 1837* (1840) *and came to this country at the age of seven* (actually nine). *He learned the printing trade in New Haven, Conn.*

He served in the Civil War in the First Connecticut heavy artillery serving under General McClellan in the Army of the Potomac. He was in 18 battles in the Civil War from May 1861 to September 1865. He enlisted as a private and came out a first lieutenant and brevet captain.

Coming west, he worked in Montana, Sacramento and San Francisco and on to Portland in 1887. He took an active interest in typographical circles, holding many offices including the presidency.

Captain O'Brien was well-known in the Oregonian *family 30 years ago in the "case days,[1]" says the article.*

When President Hoover was young, he used to drop into the printing office at Salem and watch Captain O'Brien set type. Captain O'Brien was state expert in Salem for two years, looking over books, etc.

On his ranch at Lorane, Mr. O'Brien has a horse more than 30 years old and named "Harvey" after Harvey Scott of the Oregonian.

Besides his wife, a daughter, Mrs. Catherine Hannigan, lives with him. Another daughter, Mrs. M.J. McGrath, lives in Portland. A son, William O'Brien, was with the A.E.F. (American Expeditionary Forces) *overseas and was reported missing[2].*

On February 9, 1931, a notice appeared in the newly-merged *Eugene Register-Guard.*

Capt. John O'Brien, who is 94 years old, is quite ill. His daughter, Mrs. Anna Hawkins of Seattle, is visiting him and her sister, Mrs. Katie Hannigan in Lorane.

On February 10, 1931, at 6:00 a.m., Captain John O'Brien, quietly passed away at his farm home on the Siuslaw River

---

[1] I believe this to mean that he worked in the days when type was set by hand without the use of a machine.

[2] I have not been able to find any more information on William's military service and/or MIA status, but I believe he was a casualty of World War I. He was not listed as a survivor in John's obituaries.

below Lorane with two of his daughters in attendance.

With John's passing, I will allow the 1892 *Pacific Union Printer* article to end his story...

If the laboring men of San Francisco are strong to-day; if the men of all trades see themselves the equals, socially and morally, of all other men; if they see their wives happy in pleasant homes, and their bright-faced little ones given the freedom from grinding toil that is the birthright of children, they owe it all, primarily, to Captain O'Brien. His was the hand that faltered not in the time of trial, and his the brain that saw in organization the magic that was to lift the curse of labor.

... It has been a life well spent. Mr. O'Brien has done good work for his fellows, and he bids fair to live many years longer to accomplish still more. Assuredly the record is a proud one. It is one for the young man of the craft to emulate, and for the older ones to point to as a model for all time.

And the man himself, Captain John O'Brien is too modest a man to imagine for a moment that there is anything remarkable in his career, or that he has done anything more than his simple duty as an honest man and a good citizen.

Epilogue

When John passed away, Katie stayed at the farm in Lorane. On June 20, 1936, she married David Franklin Gilbert. Everyone knew him as "Frank." Frank was the young man who worked for John occasionally on the farm. He came to Lorane in 1886 with his parents, Aaron and Rebecca Gilbert, and they were close neighbors of John.

Shortly after Frank and Katie married, he hired Clarence Roemhild of Lorane to build a new house for them on the property. I have been told that John's house had burned or

This appears to be the new house that Frank and Katie built in ~1936 to replace the original home that John built. *Courtesy of Rena Gowing*

had been torn down at some point and the new house built for the Gilberts was on the property for many years until it, too, burned.

The home that currently sits on the site near where John originally built his house, was constructed in 1972. It's where the Evan and Loretta Mann family lived for many years. When the Manns acquired the place in 1968, there was no house on it. Their son, Steven Mann, provided me with more information:

When we bought the property, it was an old homestead that had been abandoned since the last house had burned down. There had actually been two houses that burned there and they were built close to where we put in the split level house in 1972.

I can remember when we first moved there, it had the original barn and a pig shed on the south side of the creek. The driveway was also on the south side and we moved it to north side. There was also a woodshed by the stream and a root cellar. We diverted the stream water to flow through the root cellar to keep it cool in the summer.

The outhouse was located up the hill under the big cedar tree and a chicken coop was on the north side of garden. It still had portions of the picket fence around the garden area and by the henhouse.

The orchard was still producing and had some of the biggest apples I've ever seen. Looks like some of the orchard is still there.

I've always wondered if there were any records of the two previous houses and when they burned down. That would give a time frame of how long it was empty until we moved out.

I can remember the first time we looked at the property. When we bought it, we moved into a 10' x 40' single-wide trailer. We went through the big snow storm in January of 1969, living in the trailer before we built the house in 1972.

On the east side of the road there had been a sawmill and it had left a large pile of wood shavings that we used for quite a while. There is a house on that site now...

Katie O'Brien Hannigan Gilbert and Frank Gilbert on the Lorane homestead property. *Courtesy of Rena Gowing*

Katie Gilbert and friend on the homestead. *Courtesy of Rena Gowing*

Frank Gilbert, friends, Bill Moore and wife, and Marie Hannigan, Katie and Frank's only child. *Courtesy of Rena Gowing*

Hunters, Frank Gilbert, Bill Moore, and Steve Gilbert. The location may have been on Steve Gilbert's property near Lorane. *Courtesy of Rena Gowing*

Addendum

- Muster Roll
- Pension application documents
- Obituaries
- John O'Brien Death Certificate
- Grave marker

MUSTER ROLL
FOURTH REGIMENT, CONN. VOLUNTEERS

COMPANY F, OF NEW HAVEN.

NICHOLAS S. HALLENBECK, Captain.

EDWIN C. DOW, 1st Lieutenant.   GEORGE M. HARMON, 2d Lieut.

CORNELIUS C. VANALSTINE, 1st Sergeant.
RUSSELL WILCOX, 2d Sergeant.   HENRY J. HUBBARD, 4th Sergeant.
ROB'T LANGDALE, 3d   "   JOHN H. BURTON, 5th   "

WILLIAM LINCOLN, 1st Corporal.   ELLIOTT N. SMITH, 5th Corporal.
EDWIN LARRABEE, 2d   "   HERMAN B. FRENCH, 6th   "
SAM'L C. GIENNEY, 3d   "   SETH WARNER, 7th   "
JAMES A. PECK, 4th   "   WM. E. HUBBARD, 8th   "

REUBEN BLAKE, Musician.   EDWARD A. WEED, Musician.
Henry N. Emmons, Wagoner.

PRIVATES

Booth, Walter J.
Blakesley, George L.
Browning, Wm. H.
Banham, Edmond
Boardman, Henry D.
Ball, William
Bailey, Claudius A.
Bartlett, Charles,
Beardsley, Jas. J
Boyce, Daniel J.
Bodge, Andrew
Bodge, Albert
Bullivant, James
Couch, George H.
Church, Martin L.
Camden, Henry F.
Comelley, William
Chapman, Benj. K.
Chapman, Joel A.
Chapman, Jacob A.
Crowley, Dennis
Dayton, George H.
Downs, James L
Douglass, John P.
Davis, Daniel
Frivel, James
Füer, Chas. W.

Goodyear, Walstine
Hubbard, Alex. S.
Herrishaft, John K.
Hall, Samuel B.
Harris, Fred. A.
Hopper, Charles H.
Herrick, Charles H.
Hildrup, John J.
Hall, James P.
Hoyt, Henry
Johnson, Chas. P.
Johnson, Dwight
Jones, Addison C.
Kidder, Martin
Lewis, George L.
Leonard, Chas. T.
Mason, James L
Murphey, John H.
Morse, Chas. L
Miller, James J
Murray, James D.
Munson, Beers
Murray, William
Murphey, William
Newman, James H.
O'Brien, John
O'Brien, Michael
Pierson, Chas. A.

Porter, Ashel A.
Pierce, George L.
Porter, Jefferson
Patterson, Henry D.
Pelken, Charles
Phelps, Chas. W.
Reynolds, Benj.
Rudd, John P.
Rowland, Geo. H.
Rodgers, Leverett M.
Raimond, Albert C.
Robinson, Richard
Sanford, Ed-on
Sperry, Geo. P.
Shepard, Charles S.
Sanford, Charles W.
Shepard, Durell
Stone, Walter A.
Stowe, Luke
Sullivan, Melville
Sweetland, James
Simons, Geo. A.
Simons, Amos
Sneider, James
Tyler, Herman A.
Tate, William J.
Waldron, Fred. H.

John O'Brien
XC 2640256

(See reverse for explanation)

3-173.

Eastern Div.
Claim No. 1193.985.
John O'Brien,
Co. I, 1st Reg't Cav. N.Y.

Department of the Interior,
BUREAU OF PENSIONS,
Washington, D. C., November 7th, 1898.

Sir:
Will you kindly answer, at your earliest convenience, the questions enumerated below? The information is requested for future use, and it may be of great value to your family.

Very respectfully,

Mr. John O'Brien,
#374 Sixth St.
Portland, Oregon

_____, Commissioner.

No. 1. Are you a married man? If so, please state your wife's full name, and her maiden name.
Answer: Yes; Julia Agnes O'Brien; maiden name _____

No. 2. When, where, and by whom were you married? Answer: June 15, 1869; St. Mary's Cathedral, San Francisco; Father Croke.

No. 3. What record of marriage exists? Answer: My wife's certificate. Record St. Mary's Cathedral, San Francisco, Cal.

No. 4. Were you previously married? If so, please state the name of your former wife and the date and place of her death or divorce. Answer: No.

No. 5. Have you any children living? If so, please state their names and the dates of their birth. Answer: Yes. Wm. F. O'Brien, April 18, 1870, Catherine, August 1871 — she died.
Lizzie, 1873. Sin died.
Annie 1879x
Nellie 1880x
(I am a little doubtful as to days and months, as I am not at home)

Date of reply, January 5, 1899.

John O'Brien
(Signature.)

ACT OF MAY 11, 1912. S—014.

DECLARATION FOR PENSION.

THE PENSION CERTIFICATE SHOULD NOT BE FORWARDED WITH THE APPLICATION.

State of **Oregon**, County of **Lane**, ss:

On this **15** day of **June**, A. D. one thousand nine hundred and **twelve**, personally appeared before me, a **Notary Public**, within and for the county and state aforesaid, **John O'Brien**, who, being duly sworn according to law, declares that he is **71** years of age, and a resident of **Lorane**, county of **Lane**, State of **Oregon**; and that he is the identical person who was ENROLLED at **Hartford, Connecticut**, under the name of **John O'Brien**, on the **23rd** day of **May**, 1861 as a **private** in **Company F, First Regiment Connecticut Heavy Artillery**, in the service of the United States, in the **Civil War**, and was HONORABLY DISCHARGED at **Hartford, Conn.**, on the **25th** day of **September** 1865. That he also served **Reenlisted Veteran Dec. 10, 1863, in F. Company, promoted 2 Lieutenant Co. A Dec. 29 '63, 1st Lieut Co. H Nov 8 '64 Transfer to Co. D Dec 19, '64 all his service in 1st Reg. C. H. Arty, left by brevet.**

That he was not employed in the military or naval service of the United States otherwise than as stated above. That his personal description at enlistment was as follows: Height, **5** feet **7** inches; complexion, **dark**; color of eyes, **grey**; color of hair, **dark brown**; that his occupation was **printer**; that he was born **September 18, 1840**, at **County Leitrim, Ireland**.

That his several places of residence since leaving the service have been as follows: **New Haven to April '66, Montana to Sept '67, Sacramento Cal to June '69, San Francisco, Cal to June '78, Lorane, Oregon to Dec. 86, Portland Ore to April '93, Lorane Oregon since.**

That he is a pensioner under certificate No. **1,101,223**. That he has applied for pension under original No. **the same**; no other pension except under No. 1,101,223, Act Feb. 6th, 1907.

That he makes this declaration for the purpose of being placed on the pension roll of the United States under the provisions of the act of May 11, 1912.

That his post-office address is **Lorane**, county of **Lane**, State of **Oregon**.

Attest: (1) **J. Hardy Crow**   **John O'Brien**
(2) **Garfield J. Crow**

Subscribed and sworn to before me this **15** day of **June**, A. D. 1912, and I hereby certify that the contents of the above declaration were fully made known and explained to the applicant before swearing, including the words **grey '07 printer** erased, and the words _____ and that I have no interest, direct or indirect, in the prosecution of this claim.

A. W. Jackson
Notary Public for Oregon

JOHN O'BRIEN
LORANE ORE
1101223   ACT MAY

No. 1. Date and place of birth? Answer. September 18, 1840. Ireland
The name of organizations in which you served? Answer. 1st Conn. Heavy Artillery

No. 2. What was your post office at enlistment? Answer. New Haven, Conn.
No. 3. State your wife's full name and her maiden name. Julia Agnes Healy
No. 4. When, where, and by whom were you married? Answer. June 15, 1869 San Francisco Cal. in the Cathedral. Father Hay is burned down
No. 5. Is there any official or church record of your marriage? There was, but the Cathedral
If so, where? Answer. in the earth quake fire
No. 6. Were you previously married? If so, state the name of your former wife, the date of the marriage, and the date and place of her death or divorce. If there was more than one previous marriage, let your answer include all former wives. Answer. No

No. 7. If your present wife was married before her marriage to you, state the name of her former husband, the date of such marriage, and the date and place of his death or divorce, and state whether he ever rendered any military or naval service, and, if so, give name of the organization in which he served. If she was married more than once before her marriage to you, let your answer include all former husbands. Answer. No. She was single — aged 18

No. 8. Are you now living with your wife, or has there been a separation? Answer. No separation; been with me part of the time — the balance with our daughter
No. 9. State the names and dates of birth of all your children, living or dead. Answer. William F. April 19, 1870; Catherine, November, 1871; Elizabeth L. June 6, 1873; Julia, October 25, 1874 — died June 1876; Margaret, 1876 — died the same day as Julia of diphtheria; Etta Annea, August 20, 1879; Ellen, November 1, 1881. I have no record with me and am giving the children's record from memory. My eldest daughter (Mrs. Harrigan, Portland, Ore.) has my family bible and I sent her for safe keeping. I am living on my land homesteaded in 1873-1877, under the Soldiers' Act.

Date Lorane, Ore   (Signature) John O'Brien
March 24, 1915

DECLARATION FOR WIDOW'S PENSION
Act of May 1, 1920

State of __Oregon__, County of __Lane__, ss:

On this __15th__ day of __March__, 1931, before me, the undersigned, personally appeared __Julia O'Brien__, who makes the following declaration as an application for pension under the provisions of the act of Congress approved May 1, 1920.

That she is __71__ years of age, that she was born __April 3rd 1849__, at __Ireland, do not know the exact place__.

That she is the widow of __John O'Brien__, who ENLISTED __December 10, 1863__, at __Hertford Conn.__, under the name of __John O'Brien__, in F. Company Heavy Artillery as private.

DISCHARGED __Sept 25__, 1865, having served ninety days or more, or was discharged for, or died in service of the United States of a disability incurred in the service in the line of duty, during the CIVIL WAR, and who DIED __Feb. 10th__ 1931, at __Lorane, Oregon__.

That he also served in __the Civil War first as private and discharged as Corpl__ and was in 13 different engagements __to his credit, his longest siege 19 at__ and that, except as herein stated, said soldier (or sailor) was __not__ employed in the military or naval service of the United States;

THAT SHE WAS MARRIED to said soldier (or sailor) __June 25, 1869__, under the name of __Julia Haley__, at __San Francisco, Calif, at the lat__ by __Father Pindegrast__; that she had __not__ been previously married, that he had __not__ been previously married;

That neither she nor said soldier was ever married otherwise than as stated above.
That she was NOT divorced from the soldier (or sailor) and that she has NOT remarried since his death;
That the following are the ONLY children OF THE SOLDIER (or sailor) who are now living and are under sixteen years of age:

_____ born __none__, 1____, at _____
_____ born _____, 1____, at _____
_____ born _____, 1____, at _____
_____ born _____, 1____, at _____
_____ born _____, 1____, at _____

That she __did not__ serve in the Army, Navy, Marine Corps, or Coast Guard of the United States between April 6, 1917, and July 2, 1921, or at any time during said period.

That __no__ member of her family served in the Army, Navy, Marine Corps, or Coast Guard of the United States between April 6, 1917, and July 2, 1921, or at any time during said period.

That she has __not__ heretofore applied for pension, the number of her former claim being _____; that said soldier (or sailor) was __a pensioner__, the number of his pension certificate being # __1101223__.

(1) __Vivian Longfellow__ (Signature of first witness)
__Cottage Grove, Oregon__ (Address of first witness)

(2) __E L Lockwood__ (Signature of second witness)
__Cottage Grove Oregon__ (Address of second witness)

__Julia O'Brien__ (Claimant's signature in full)
__1401 8 Ave - West__
__Seattle Wash__ (Claimant's address in full)

Subscribed and sworn to before me this __15th__ day of __March__ 1931, and I hereby certify that the contents of the above declaration were fully made known and explained to the applicant before swearing, including the words _____ erased, and the words _____ added; and that I have no interest, direct or indirect, in the prosecution of this claim.

[L. S.]

__S J Shinn__ (Signature)
Notary Public for Oregon (Official character)

Eugene Register-Guard
February 10, 1931

LORANE CIVIL WAR VETERAN IS DEAD

Captain John O'Brien, 93, Once Prominent As Oregon Leader

Captain John O'Brien, Civil War officer, and for many years Oregon newspaper man and labor leader, died Tuesday morning at his farm home on the Siuslaw river below Lorane. He was 93 years of age.

Captain O'Brien was born at Connaught, Ireland, September 18, 1839, and came to the United States with his parents in 1843, settling in Connecticut, where he grew to manhood and was educated. At the outbreak of the Civil War he enlisted in the Union army as a private and at the close was the captain of Company F, First Connecticut heavy artillery.

Following the close of the war, Captain O'Brien moved to Oregon. He joined the staff of the Portland Oregonian and was for many years a reporter for that paper. In 1895 he founded the old Portland Daily Sun, which circulated throughout Oregon for a number of years.

In addition to his work as a journalist, Captain O'Brien was a leader in labor work in Oregon, and for several years was the state president of the American Federation of Labor.

In 1907, then 70 years of age, Captain O'Brien retired and moved to his farm near Lorane, where he lived until the time of his death. He is survived by his widow, Mrs. Julia O'Brien, and three daughters, Mrs. Katharine Hannigan of Lorane, Mrs. M. J. McGrath of Portland, and Mrs. A. H. Hankins of Seattle. He was a member of the Eugene Masonic lodge number 11.

The funeral service will be held at the Veatch chapel Thursday afternoon at 2 o'clock with the members of the Eugene Masonic lodge in charge. The body will be taken to Portland for interment.

Funeral Notices

O'BRIEN—Funeral services for the late Capt. John O'Brien, age 93, of Lorane, who passed away on Feb. 10th, will be held Thursday, Feb. 12 at 2 p. m. Masonic lodge will have charge of the service. Remains will be taken to Memorial hall in Portland for interment. Arrangements in care of Veatch Funeral Home, Phone 112.

[Oregon State Board of Health Certificate of Death for John O'Brien]

Pioneer Oregonian Reporter Passes at 93

ONE of the oldest of old-time newspaper men of Oregon passed with the recent death of Capt. John O'Brien, 93 years old, veteran of the Civil war and a reporter on the *Oregonian* for many years after the close of the war. In 1895 Captain O'Brien founded the Portland *Daily Sun*, which circulated throughout Oregon for a number of years. Captain O'Brien was a leader in Oregon labor circles, having been for several years president of the federation of labor in this state. He retired at 70 to the farm near Lorane where he passed the last 23 years of his life. He is survived by his widow and three daughters. Captain O'Brien was a native of Ireland. He came to the United States with his parents in 1843. His title of captain was won in the field as a heavy artillerist.

Oregon Exchange magazine

Portland Oregonian
February 11, 1931

CIVIL WAR OFFICER DIES

CAPTAIN O'BRIEN ONCE ON THE OREGONIAN.

Ex-President of State Federation of Labor 93 Years of Age at Death.

EUGENE, Or., Feb. 10.-(Special.)- Captain John O'Brien, 93, civil war officer and for many years Oregon newspaper man and labor leader, died today at his farm home on the Siuslaw river below Lorane.

Captain O'Brien was born in Connaught, Ireland, September 18, 1839, and came to the United States with his parents in 1843. At the outbreak of the civil war he enlisted in the Union army as a private and at the close was the captain of company F, 1st Connecticut heavy artillery.

Following the close of the war Captain O'Brien moved to Oregon. He joined the staff of The Oregonian, Portland, and was for many years a printer for that paper. In 1895 he founded the old Portland Daily Sun, which circulated throughout Oregon for a number of years.

In addition to his work as a journalist, Captain O'Brien was a leader in labor work in Oregon, and for several years was the state president of the American Federation of Labor.

In 1907, then 70 years of age, Captain O'Brien retired to his farm near Lorane, where he lived until the time of his death. He is survived by the widow, Mrs. Julia O'Brien, and three daughters, Mrs. Katharine Hannigan of Lorane, Mrs. M. J. McGrath of Portland and Mrs. A. H. Hankins of Seattle. He was a Mason.

The birth year information provided for these articles as well as his death certificate by John's daughter, Anna, is incorrect as are the dates on the name marker where his remains were interred at the Riverview Abbey Mausoleum and Crematory in Portland, Oregon.

Bibliography

Books and Publications

Billings, Harry (1963) *The History of the Montana Typographical Conference*; Montana Historical Society.

Dyer, F.H. (1908) *Compendium of the War of the Rebellion,* Volume 1; The Dyer Publishing Co.

Editor (1892) "Captain John O'Brien;" Pacific Union Printer newsletter, San Francisco Typographical Union No. 21;Volume V, No. 3; San Francisco, CA

Editor, *Southern Arizona News-Examiner*, (newspaper)

Editor, "Elmer Ellsworth;" U.S. National Park Service.

Editors (1967) *A Study of the History of the International Typographical Union 1852 to 1963.* Executive Council, Colorado Springs, Colorado

Edwards, Owen (April 2011) "The Death of Colonel Ellsworth;" Smithsonian.

Edwards, Pat (2014) *OREGON'S MAIN STREET: U.S. Highway 99 "The Folk History"*; Groundwaters Publishing, LLC.

Edwards, Patricia Ann, O'Hearn, Nancy and Hing, Marna (2006) *From Sawdust and Cider to Wine; A History of Lorane, Oregon and the Siuslaw Valley; Groundwaters* Publishing, LLC.

Gompers, S. (1925) *From Seventy Years of Labor*, E.P. Dotton, publisher.

Gompers, S.,editor (July 1912) *American Federalist*, Official Magazine of the American Federation of Labor.

Harper, Hal (1967) *A Bulwark of Freedom: The Story of the International Typographical Union.*

Klare, G. (October 5, 2001) "Captain John O'Brien," on-line newspaper at nwLaborPress.org.

Lipset, S.M., Trow, M.A. and Coleman, J.S. (1956) *Union Democracy: The Internal Politics of the International Typographical Union*, Volume 14; The Free Press, 455 pgs.

Niven, J. (1965) *Connecticut for the Union: The Role of the State in the Civil War*; Yale University Press.

Schreiner, M. Murray (1952) *The Montana Magazine of History*, Vol. 2 No. 4; Montana Historical Society; pp 33-42

Taylor, J.C. and Hatfield, S.P. (1893) *History of the First Connecticut Artillery: and of the Siege Trains of the Armies Operating Against Richmond*, 1862-1865; Press of the Case, Lockwood & Brainard Co., Hartford, CT.

Timberlake, Jr., Richard H. (1997) "Panic of 1893." In Glasner, David; Cooley, Thomas F. *Business Cycles and Depressions: an Encyclopedia.* New York: Garland Publishing.

Tracy, G.A. (1913) *The History of the Typographical Union;* International Typographical Union.

Websites

http://battleoffallingwaters.com/battleinfo.html (Falling Waters Battlefield)
http://www.u-s-history.com/pages/h3903.html (A History of Portland, Oregon)
http://www.press.uchicago.edu/Misc/Chicago/317749.html (New York riots)
http://www.helenahistory.org/index.htm (Helena as She Was)
http://lettersfromcharleygoodyear.weebly.com/index.html
http://lettersfromcharleygoodyear.weebly.com/john-obrien.html
https://en.wikipedia.org/wiki/Peninsula_Campaign
https://en.wikipedia.org/wiki/William_J._Hardee
https://www.findagrave.com/memorial/
https://www.ancestry.com/
https://en.wikipedia.org/wiki/Elmer_E._Ellsworth
https://eh.net/encyclopedia/the-depression-of-1893/ (Depression of 1893)
https://www.hmdb.org/Marker.asp?Marker=8029 (Fort Lyon explosion)
https://en.wikipedia.org/wiki/Copperhead_(politics)
https://www.legendsofamerica.com/we-chicagojoe/

Newspapers

1888
- April 10; *The Morning Oregonian*, Portland, OR
- April 25; *The Morning Oregonian*, Portland, OR
- April 29; *The Sunday Oregonian*, Portland, OR
- July 10; *The Morning Oregonian*, Portland, OR
- September 24; *The Morning Oregonian*, Portland, OR
- December 21; *The Morning Oregonian*, Portland, OR

1889
- January 7; T*The Morning Oregonian*, Portland, OR
- February 27; *The Morning Oregonian*, Portland, OR
- June 30; *The Morning Oregonian*, Portland, OR

1890
- April 18; *The Morning Astorian*, Astoria, OR
- May 2; *The Albany Democrat*, Albany, OR
- May 14; *The Statesman Journal*, Salem, OR
- May 17; *The Morning Astorian*, Astoria, OR
- June 4; *The Statesman Journal*, Salem, OR

1891
- October 13; *The Statesman Journal*, Salem, OR

1892
- January 22; *The Weekly Oregon Statesman*, Salem, OR
- May 23; *The Daily Capital Journal*, Salem, OR
- May 25; *The Dalles Chronicle*, The Dalles, OR
- December 3; *The Eugene Guard*, Eugene, OR

1893
- May 23; *The Eugene Guard*, Eugene, OR
- July 19; *The Daily Capital Journal*, Salem, OR
- November 4; *The Dalles Times-Mountaineer*, The Dalles, OR (quoting from the *Salem Independent*)

1894
- February 24; *The Daily Capital Journal*, Salem, OR
- February 26; *The Albany Daily Democrat*, Albany, OR
- March 9; *The Weekly Oregon Statesman*, Salem, OR
- April 17; *The Daily Capital Journal*, Salem, OR
- April 17; *The Morning Astorian*, Astoria, OR
- April 18; *The Dalles Chronicle*, The Dalles, OR
- April 18; *The Morning Astorian*, Astoria, OR
- April 19; *The Lincoln County Leader*, Toledo, OR

June 2; *The Morning Astorian*, Astoria, OR
June 8; *The Weekly Oregon Statesman*, Salem, OR
July 7; *The Dalles Times-Mountaineer*, The Dalles, OR
July 10; *The Statesman Journal*, Salem, OR
October 12; *The St. Helens Mist*, St. Helens OR
1899
April 15; *The Daily Capital Journal*, Salem, OR
May 12; *The Daily Capital Journal*, Salem, OR
1901
December 3; *The Morning Register*, Eugene, OR
1903
May 8; *The Camas Prairie Chronicle*, Cottonwood, Idaho
October 3; *The Eugene Guard*, Eugene, OR
1904
February 27; *The Oregon Daily Journal*, Portland, OR
1907
April 12; *The Morning Register*, Eugene, OR
1912
December 26; *The Oregon Daily Journal*, Portland, OR
1922
October 14; *The Morning Register*, Eugene, OR
1928
July 18; T*The Eugene Guard*, Eugene, OR
July 28; *The Morning Register*, Eugene, OR
1930
January 20; *The Eugene Guard*, Eugene, OR, quoting from an earlier article in the Oregon Labor Press
1931
February 9; *The Eugene Guard*, Eugene, OR
February 10; *The Eugene Guard*, Eugene, OR
February 11; *The Oregonian*, Portland, OR
1995
November 10; *The Oregonian*, Portland, OR (Garry Frank)

Documents

Declaration for Pension filed by John O'Brien on June 15, 1912
Pension Application filed by John O'Brien on March 24, 1915
Pension Application filed by John O'Brien on November 18, 1898
Widow's Pension Application filed by Julia O'Brien on March 18, 1931

Other Resources

Department of Interior, Bureau of Pensions
Guides to National Archives Microfilm Publications: Civil War Compiled Service Records
John Dwyer, descendant of Captain John O'Brien
Montana Historical Society Research Center, Helena, MT
Northwest Labor Press
Oregon Marriage Index, 1855-1919
The National Archives for Pension files and Military Records
Vital Records; New Haven, CT; marriage records

Other Books by Pat Edwards

Edwards, P.A., O'Hearn, N. and Hing, M (1987) *Sawdust and Cider to Wine; A History of Lorane, Oregon and the Siuslaw Valley* . Out of print

Edwards, P. (2006) *From Sawdust and Cider to Wine*

Brew, J. (2013) *OREGON'S MAIN STREET: U.S. Highway 99 "The Stories"* (Pat Edwards, editor & collaborator)

Edwards, P. (2014) *OREGON'S MAIN STREET: U.S. Highway 99 "The Folk History"* (Jo-Brew, collaborator)

Edwards, P. (2017) *The Baileys of Bailey Hill*

~~~~

Groundwaters Publishing, LLC annual anthologies produced by Pat Edwards; Jennifer Chambers, co-editor:
- *Groundwaters 2015; An Anthology*
- *Groundwaters 2016; An Anthology*
- *Groundwaters 2017; An Anthology*

All books can be ordered on-line at
https://allthingslorane.com/published-books/

To Contact the Author...

Pat Edwards
P.O. Box 50, Lorane, OR 97451
edwards@groundwaterspublishing.com
http://allthingslorane.com

Please leave feedback on Amazon.com!

Groundwaters Publishing, LLC
P.O. Box 50
Lorane, OR 97451
http://groundwaterspublishing.com

www.ingramcontent.com/pod-product-compliance
Lightning Source LLC
Chambersburg PA
CBHW070429010526
44118CB00014B/1962